Freedom From Fear
by Jeanne Hall

A Testimony to
The Power of God in the Life of
Korean War Hero
Robert S. Durham

**Based on letters
to his grandchildren**

New Messenger Writing and Publishing

Freedom From Fear

by Jeanne Hall

A Testimony to the Power of God
In the life of Korean War Hero
Robert S. Durham

PUBLISHED NOVEMBER 1995
ISBN 1888338-00-8

New Messenger Books / Religious Division
PO Box 2463
Knoxville, TN 37901

New Messenger Books may be purchased for educational, religious, business or promotional use. For information, write to the above address or phone 423-428-0389. Use the same address to inquire about publication of your book.

COVER: BOB DURHAM PHOTO (COLOR) BY PAUL EFIRD.
KOREAN MEMORIAL PHOTO BY SCOTT BOATRIGHT.
COVER DESIGN BY BRIAN BURGESS AT HART GRAPHICS.

Editor's Note: In keeping with the wishes of the author, all nouns and pronouns referring to God are in upper case, as are references to the Bible. All Biblical quotations prior to page 99 are from the *King James Version*. For reasons that will be clear to readers, all those on and following page 99 are from *The Living Bible*, copyright 1971. Used by permission of Tyndale House Publishers, Inc., Wheaton, Illinois, 60189. All rights reserved. For a discussion of other stylistic conventions followed in this book, see "Author's Note," page 127.

Faith Under Fire . . .

"Please don't leave us! We'll all be killed." Bob looked down into the begging eyes of a blood-soaked Marine.

He wanted to go. He had orders to go. Every muscle, nerve, and tendon was poised to escape this death trap. He was more afraid than he had ever been in his life. He didn't want to die. He especially didn't want to be wounded and crippled for the rest of his life. But the power of the Holy Spirit—that Power and Shield of Faith that had been within his heart since childhood to help overcome his fear—was strong within him now. Bob decided instantly that he had to stay where he was and defend his brothers. He prayed more earnestly than he had ever prayed that God would help him get the wounded men back down the hill to safety. Again the words of God came to his mind and heart, and again they gave him strength to stand:

The Lord is my light and my salvation; whom shall I fear? **(Psalm 27:1)** . . .

3

This book is dedicated to my wife, Margaret,
who has been a helpmate and a blessing to me,
and who has supported and assisted the preparation
of this manuscript with patience and prayer;
to my daughters, Becky and Diane;
my grandchildren, Lyndi, Kathleen, Emily and Daniel,
who are my life's treasures, inspiration and legacy,
and to Matthew Parsons, who is the son I never had—
my daily challenge and daily joy.

—*Robert S. Durham*

***

**Winner of the Silver Star
For Courage During Combat**

Contents

Introduction

by Dr. Larry W. Fields
Pastor of Central Baptist Church of Bearden

For the past nine years I have had the privilege to serve as Bob Durham's pastor at the Central Baptist Church of Bearden in Knoxville, Tennessee. I am pleased that he has felt God leading him to put his life story in written words. With refreshing honesty and openness, he demonstrates God's hand in his life during good times and bad.

Using Bible verses to reveal the power of God's love, he weaves his life story through childhood, his Korean war experiences, his successes and failures in family life, and the development of a Single Adult Ministry in his church that today has over 300 enrolled.

His personal testimony concerning God's constant love and support will be a strong witness to others who struggle with the realities of life. By allowing us to look over his shoulder during all these years, he reminds us that "God is a very present help." I am confident that you will benefit and be inspired for sharing this personal pilgrimage.

September 29, 1995
Knoxville, Tennessee

1/ The Beginning

*H*ow strange and wonderful that God, even before the foundation of the world was laid, had purposed in His heart the creation of all that was to be.

In the beginning—in that far-distant, infinitely powerful explosion of His creative nature, filling eon after eon in the emptiness that preceded even space as we know it—God created all. In His imagination originated each star and all its planets, each planet and all its incredibly complex systems, each living thing, plant and animal, from microscopic single cells to the largest redwood trees, the mammoths and the whales.

And within the intimate and mysterious womb of God's consummate, holy love, each human being's unique personal existence was ordained, and each person's role assigned in God's Great Plan that will, ultimately, result in the perfect union when we shall all be One—at last complete and free in loving Him and loving each other and loving ourselves. "Then," says God's Holy Word, "Shall we know, even as we are known."

But the history of humankind is a long record of ignorance and selfish misunderstanding. We frequently have misread the prophecies and watched and hoped for warrior-kings who would lead us to fame and fortune while making this world perfect ... for us. When our expectations were not met, we stoned the prophets and crucified the Messiah.

No one expected God to come to the earth so humbly—as a baby born to a carpenter's wife. He came at an inconvenient time in a most unlikely place, a dusty stable on the outskirts of a poor country town. No one would even have noticed the birth, except that God sent a special bright star as a sign of the extraordinary event.

Why, we wonder, were there only three out of the whole world at that time wise enough to ignore those who called them foolish and go on to seek the origin of that wondrous star. God also sent His own angel messengers to announce the Messiah's birth—not to the kings and politicians and religious leaders, but to a group of uneducated working men of that time—lonely shepherds resting with their flocks. Filled with wonder, the shepherds immediately went to find the Holy Child and worship Him. But soon most people had forgotten the wonder of Christ's birth, and it was many years before His power and glory were known throughout the land.

Humans haven't changed much in the centuries since. If a child is born in our own family, we as parents and grandparents may briefly comprehend the miracle of that new life with all its potential for good and evil, productivity and pain. We wonder, as Mary and Joseph must have wondered, will he be strong and wise and handsome and brave? Will she be strong and wise and good and beautiful? What will the world bring for this child in the years ahead?

Or the wonderings may be more personal and more practical. Can I afford to care for this child? Will I be a good parent? How will this child affect my life?

* * *

Questions like these surely were in the minds of another poor, young couple when their boy child was born, centuries later and half a world away from Bethlehem.

The tall, lanky, young farmer and his plump, young wife must have asked themselves the same old human questions, as she agonized with the pain of childbirth, and he waited while their baby son was born. Hardly anyone outside the family noticed the boy's birth. No one except them saw anything special about their baby. Only God saw the potential power and glory of the life that began in a rundown building in the dusty, small town of Springfield, Tennessee on July 10, 1931.

The boy took after his mother, Bessie. He had her dark, fine, curly hair and brown eyes, dark and deep. She loved him at once. Holding him in her arms as he drank the milk of her breasts, she opened her heart to him and he became her own. She rejoiced in his perfect, small body and saw in him an end to the long days of boredom and loneliness. She named him Robert Sidney, for both of his grandfathers. From that moment until her death she always called him "my Bobby."

Fathers at that time were outsiders to the birthing and were banned from the delivery. Their chief and proper contributions were getting the expectant mother to the doctor on time, transporting mother and child safely home on the appointed day and paying the bills promptly.

When this young father, named Bunyan, first saw his baby boy, the weight of that responsibility must have been uppermost in his mind. He was a sharecropper's son, living in a rented house in one of the poorest towns of a poverty-stricken Southern state struggling to recover from the Great Depression. He must have had mixed feelings about the arrival of a child after only a year of marriage. Masculine pride over fathering a son might have mingled with fear that the baby would receive all the love and attention of his new wife. It may have been hard to rejoice over another mouth to feed and more bills to pay on a salary that already seemed scarcely enough.

It has always been a truism in the South that to know the person you must know the family. Not only the father, but the father's father and his father's family. As far back as anyone remembered, Bunyan's family, the Durham family, had been strong, hard-working yeomen of the soil. They were sharecroppers who tilled the earth, growing and harvesting plentiful crops on land belonging to other, wealthier men. Some said the need to own property was not in the Durham blood. With property came taxes and the weight of responsibility for the property and those it supported.

Bunyan's family, and Bunyan himself, valued personal freedom more than property. As they saw it, their lack of ownership gave them independence. It left them free to leave the land after the harvest was in, although they seldom did. They loved the land and the life-giving cycle of growth and harvest much more than those who lived in cities and merely owned land. They loved the spaces of field and sky around them, the changes of the seasons, the feel and smell of good soil worked properly, the freedom to choose what tasks should be done today and what should be left until tomorrow.

In town they felt hemmed in and self-conscious. In the country they could live as they wanted to live. Loyalty to the family and to the land was strong in the Durham family. As sharecroppers, they were not expected to be the pillars of the church, run for political office, or make large donations of time and money for the public good. Despite limited means, they could do some of these things if they wanted, but the burden of expectation was not there.

Bunyan's father, "Pap," and mother, "Mam," taught their thirteen children (seven girls and six boys) of the life they knew. They taught them how to grow good crops in the rock-laden, red-clay soil of the Middle Tennessee hills; how to work long hard hours without tiring or complaining; to give an honest accounting of farm expenses and returns and to keep the farmhands, colored and white, busy and contented with their lot in life. What a person did beyond that, so long as it didn't involve breaking the law or vary too much from the local custom, the Durham children learned, was their own business. It was a hard life, but an honorable one. Bunyan loved it.

Bobby's mother, Bessie Holliman, was a city girl. Her family lived in Springfield, a small town on the outskirts of Nashville. Her father held a job with the city. It was a minor political appointment resulting from her father's fortunate and diligent campaigning for a friend who was subsequently elected to the city council. Bessie was one of five children, four daughters and one son. Her parents were proud of the family and their position in town. Her father loved and indulged all of his children, especially his girls.

Although he refused to learn to drive "new-fangled" automobiles, he understood that women like to go places and do things. So he bought a car and hired a driver to take his wife and daughters wherever they wanted to go. He believed in education. His son became an engineer and, when Bessie proved to be a good student with an interest in scholarship and not much prospect for an early marriage, he saw to it that she could attend college, which was unusual for girls of that era.

No one remembers exactly how Bessie Holliman and Bunyan Durham met, fell in love and married each other. It was a tradition in the Durham family that each of the boys spend some time serving a sort of apprenticeship with an uncle in Nashville who had a pipefitting business. This was a type of Depression-era job-security insurance, so that if the boys were not able to farm, they could possibly find a pipefitting job in town. Bunyan may have been in Nashville visiting his uncle about the time Bessie was finishing her second year of college.

She was a smart girl with a lively, sardonic sense of humor, but she was short and overweight from early childhood onward. By her second dateless year in college, she must have been wondering if she would ever be asked to marry. Perhaps she and some college girlfriends went out to one of the Nashville honky-tonks that were as plentiful then as now. Maybe there she met the tall, quiet farm boy, Bunyan. Maybe she sang with the crowd as he played the piano. Maybe they talked some after he'd had a few drinks. Maybe she liked the way his hungry eyes watched her and the way he held her when he finally asked her to dance.

Bunyan may have thought the dark-eyed, full-fleshed young woman would warm his heart and his bed and make a good, sturdy farm wife. Bessie may have thought it better to be a mother and wife—wanted by this strong, silent man—than to be a college-educated spinster. At any rate, Bunyan asked her to marry, and she accepted.

To support his wife and please her, Bunyan took a job in the nearby town of Springfield, working in a flour mill that belonged to a wealthy man named Tony Dowling. The pay was small, and there were few responsibilities, but Bunyan worked hard, as he had been taught. He was a good craftsman, too, and was able to make minor mechanical repairs that helped keep the old machinery of the mill operating.

Their small rental house felt cozy and warm to the young couple in love, and, when work was over, there was a little money and enough time to have fun together. Later they laughed, remembering that they owned a piano before they owned a bed, and their evenings together in those honeymoon days were filled with music and love.

Bessie was already a Christian when they married. To please her and to show his determination to be a solid, respectable husband, Bunyan joined the church and was baptized early in their marriage. They attended church regularly, and God blessed this first year together. Neither of them worried much about the future, at least not until Bobby was born.

Old photographs contrast life in town and country. Left, Bobby with parents, Bunyan and Bessie Durham in 1931. Right, about 1935.

2/ Growing Up

They tried to be good parents in the manner they had been taught by their own mothers and fathers. To Bessie, that meant taking good care of the infant, keeping him warm and dry and filled with milk. Drying his tears and holding him close when he cried gave her as much pleasure as it did the baby. To Bunyan, being a good parent meant being a good worker, trying to get ahead at the mill, and trying to stay out of the way of a sometimes tired and cranky wife and crying baby at home. He wanted to give the boy a good life—which to him meant a life in the country, on the farm.

When Bobby was about a year old, the mill owner, Mr. Dowling, bought a large tract of land in the country outside of Springfield. He offered strong, hard-working Bunyan the job of overseeing the land. In addition to a salary increase and a percentage of the harvest, the job included a large, old house to live in on the farm, a car to drive and land on which to grow all the vegetables they wanted for their personal use. Bunyan saw it as a wonderful opportunity and accepted immediately. Bessie tried to see it the same way, but her heart sank at the thought of leaving her family and friends and the church in town. She had never lived on a farm and never wanted to.

Nevertheless, the offer was too good to turn down, and the little family moved to the country. The house was one of those old farmhouses that had been built on to many times through the years to hold large families with lots of children. It had once been a fine house, but had stood ramshackle and abandoned for many years. All its rooms were filled with cobwebs and dust and, Bessie suspected, rats, bats, squirrels and God only knew what other dangerous and disgusting "critters." Not to mention ghosts!

The big house was heated only by fireplaces in each of the main rooms. There was no electricity, no indoor plumbing, no running water, not even a well. Water came from a cistern that caught rainwater from the roof. When the cistern went dry, they hauled water from a spring.

With little furniture and no desire to clean out and use all of those dusty old rooms, Bessie and Bunyan settled into the four main rooms on the first floor of the old house. The walls and floors creaked at night, and Bessie could hear (or imagine that she heard) through the high ceilings and uninsulated walls, scurrying feet of the critters she felt sure lived in rooms she never had the courage or desire to explore.

Bessie hated living in the country. She hated the farm, the old ramshackle house, the lack of electricity and all those modern conveniences she had always taken for granted when living in town. She missed the coziness of her little house and the closeness of her family and friends. She discovered that on a farm the work is never really done. There was seldom any time or energy left, after working dawn to dark, for the music and fun that she and Bunyan and baby Bobby used to share in the evenings. She also missed her church, because, once they moved to the farm, they stopped attending the small Baptist church in Springfield.

Bunyan was disappointed that his wife couldn't share his excitement and pride at being the manager and boss of such a fine, large estate. More and more he withdrew from the unhappy wife and child and spent all his time and energy making the farm a success. This was the life he loved, the work he was good at, and he desperately wanted his family to be proud of him and to share his happiness in the farm. But he was not a man who could express his thoughts and feelings, and he never found the way to make his wishes come true.

Bessie could not be happy on the farm. As much as possible, she tried to protect herself and her Bobby from what she considered the dirt and the dangers of farming. As children are apt to do, the little boy sensed the emotional distress of his mother and the new atmosphere of tension and unhappiness in the house. Bessie often had to help in the fields and garden, and, since there was no one to call on for babysitting, she sometimes left the two-year-old boy alone in his crib in the big old house.

In those days, when rural crime was practically nonexistent and hardly anyone in the rural South even locked their front door, this was not as negligent as it now sounds. But it was devastating to the boy already feeling threatened and insecure because of his mother's tears and anger and his father's withdrawal and rejection. So many days and hours Bobby must have screamed and cried in fear and loneliness, with no one there to hear. Gradually he learned that the crying did not cause his parents to return and comfort him. So he learned to control the tears, to entertain himself with his own growing imagination and to gather comfort from the familiar things in the house—the furniture, the piano, the bed and his mother's and daddy's clothes. Gradually he learned that his parents would, after all, return; that the abandonment he felt was not complete or permanent.

Bessie tried to help by teaching him that he was never truly alone, that God was always there watching over him. She read to him from the Bible at night and taught him the prayer all Southern children used to learn at their mother's knee:

> *Now I lay me down to sleep;*
> *I pray thee, Lord, my soul to keep.*
> *If I should die before I wake,*
> *I pray thee, Lord, my soul to take.*

Near his crib, she hung a picture of a beautiful angel watching over two small children, and she told him that

God's guardian angels watched over her Bobby too. She taught him about Jesus and assured him that Jesus loved him.

Despite her brave and comforting words, Bobby could feel her fear whenever she left him or whenever Bunyan left the two of them in the house alone. Gradually, Bobby learned not to cry, but, like his mother, he could not learn to be unafraid. At night, when the creaking and scurrying sounds of the house kept the boy from sleeping, Bessie often pulled his crib close beside their bed and held his hand in the dark, as much to comfort herself as to comfort him. The house was always a scary place for both of them.

Bunyan didn't share their fear. He loved the farm life. He loved watching things grow and took pride in the fine fields of corn and tobacco standing straight and green in the Tennessee sunshine. He was proud of his ability to manage the large estate and was delighted to have plenty of money and plenty of equipment to work the land. He was a good farmer, a good worker, a good foreman, and he liked using his mechanical abilities to keep the farm machinery in working order.

A black family lived on the farm about a mile and a half down the dusty, unpaved road from the Durhams' house. Rachel and Ben and their older children worked as farmhands and, once Bessie came to know and trust them, often kept Bobby at their house when Bessie and Bunyan went into town for groceries or an occasional evening out at a local tavern or "honky tonk." Ben and Rachel had lots of children, and there were always sisters, brothers, cousins, uncles, aunts and friends coming and going. There was plenty of noise and confusion, laughing and singing, and games. Bobby learned that there was always some fun going on at Ben and Rachel's house, and he enjoyed the warmth and security of staying with them. The little black children of that household were like his brothers and sisters. They became his first playmates, first friends and first sweethearts. When he was at Ben and Rachel's house, Bobby was never lonely and he was never afraid.

Bobby and his mother Bessie are shown standing in front of the rambling old farmhouse that was so frightening and lonely when Bunyan was away.

3/ The Revelation

Bessie and Bunyan worked hard on the farm for many years. They generally worked from daylight to dark six days a week. As a concession to Bessie, they often went dancing on Saturday nights and slept late on Sunday mornings. Church was no longer a part of their lives.

Bobby continued to be a lonely, fearful child. He was always afraid at home, especially when, as he grew older, he was left alone at night while his parents went for their Saturday night "honky-tonking." Always the house seemed to fill with awful, unidentifiable noises. He even grew to be afraid when he was playing outside the house, although he was too fearful to wander very far.

One day when he was about four or five years old and was left alone as usual playing in the yard, he heard a new, strange noise coming from the bushes nearby. Thoughts of monsters, tigers, bears, criminals and horrible, unknown dangers that could hurt or kill him filled Bobby with terror. He was too afraid to move, but suddenly the fear simply went away. He never learned what made the noise, but an unseen presence seemed to shield him from anything evil that might be there and even from the thought or fear of anything evil. He knew in his trusting heart, that Jesus was real and was there with him at that moment, loving him and protecting him from anything that could bring him harm. He felt the presence of an angel like the one he had seen in the picture in his room. He *knew* that the angel was sheltering him with wonderful wings, guarding him from any possible danger.

For perhaps the first time in his young life, he felt totally secure, protected, unafraid and loved. From that moment, he *knew* that Jesus was real and that God was always near, guarding him against all harm. It was a revelation that he was too young to explain, too young to fully understand, but not too young to *know* through the faith of his innocent heart.

Much later, as a teenager, he was able to find and read the powerful scriptures expressing God's love and care that he came to know through his experience that day. Psalms of the Old Testament are filled with assurances that God does not want His children to be prisoners of fear and anxiety and that all who trust in Him are totally safe and secure in His hands.

> *The Lord is my light and my salvation; whom shall I fear? The Lord is the strength of my life; of whom shall I be afraid? When the wicked, even mine*

enemies and my foes, came upon me to eat up my flesh, they stumbled and fell. **(Psalm 27:1-3)**

Because thou hast made the Lord, which is my refuge, even the most High, thy habitation, there shall no evil befall thee; neither shall any plague come nigh thy dwelling. For he shall give his angels charge over thee, to keep thee in all thy ways. (For the Lord says) Because he hath set his love upon me, therefore will I deliver him: I will set him on high, because he hath known my name. He shall call upon me, and I will answer him: I will be with him in trouble; I will deliver him and honour him. **(Psalm 91: 9-11, 14-15)**

Later in life, when Bobby came to know and love the New Testament, he found it also to be filled with God's assurances that He will faithfully guard and care for those who trust in Him.

Who shall separate us from the love of Christ? Shall tribulation, or distress, or persecution, or famine, or nakedness, or peril, or sword? Nay, in all these things we are more than conquerors through him that loved us. **(Romans 8:35-37)**

As a child not yet able to read, Bobby had not heard these scriptural promises. But from this time forward, God's overwhelming, peace-giving love was revealed directly to his innocent heart and mind. The fearful child was given the gift of faith—the shield of faith—a faith he could not yet express in words, but an unshakable, subconscious faith that would remain with him, assuring him that he was guarded and blessed by God, and that God had a special purpose for his life. With that faith came freedom from fear. Satan would continue to attack him with fear and anxiety throughout life, just as Satan attacks all of us, but Bobby would always know that, through faith and trust in God, he could overcome the fear.

* * *

In the ten or more years that the Durhams lived on the farm, the family never attended church. Bobby's mama and daddy worked hard all week—most days from sunup to sundown—for six days, and then on Saturday night they would go dancing. On Sunday mornings they always slept late. Sometimes they would take Bobby along on their Saturday night outings, and he would fall asleep in the car or in a booth in the back, or upstairs over a honky tonk. And sometimes—his favorite times—he would stay with Ben and Rachel and their big, happy family.

Sunday was always the highlight of the week for Bobby. Most of all he enjoyed having his mama or daddy read the Sunday comics (which Southerners called "the funny papers" in those days). Then they would all get in the car and go to his daddy's parents' farm for a big Sunday lunch. All of his daddy's brothers and sisters and their spouses and children would be there.

Bobby loved the gathering of aunts, uncles, cousins, parents and grandparents, and the warm feeling of belonging to the big family. It never was quite as warm and happy or as much fun as Ben and Rachel's big noisy family, but it gave him a sense of his place in the world—a feeling of security and responsibility too.

All the women would help Mam cook and serve the big dinner. The men of the family sat around with Pap drinking, smoking, chewing tobacco, playing horseshoes or just talking—mostly crops and county politics. The children, all cousins, would play games and hide and quarrel and make lots of noise until called down by the adults.

One thing that both the adults and children enjoyed was the telling of ghost stories. This area of Tennessee was famous for "the Bell Witch," a "haint" whose existence has been documented in many books and articles. The Durham men and women alike never tired of telling tales of how this or that famous person had visited the old mansion haunted by the Bell Witch and had *seen the witch in person!* These stories were taken as the absolute Gospel truth by all the children of the family, and most of them thought of the tales and shivered as they huddled under the covers each Sunday night. For a fearful and sensitive child like Bobby, these old ghost tales magnified the fears he already had about their old farm house being haunted by evil spirits.

* * *

Bobby, being one of the younger and smaller cousins, never got to be the leader or the favorite cowboy hero in their make-believe games. Sometimes he preferred to just hang around the edges where the men gathered and watch what they did. He could hardly wait to grow up, so that he could smoke and chew and drink and spit and toss the big horseshoes as they did.

Often there was music, because all the Durham children played the piano or some other musical instrument, and there was a love of music throughout the family. The Sunday gatherings were always a sort of family holiday, and on each official holiday, such as Easter or Christmas, the gatherings were even more special.

When World War II began, Bobby's daddy was drafted into the Army. However, he had a bad case of stomach ulcers and was classified 4-F because of that disability, so he did not have to go to war. But the war affected everyone, and it changed their peaceful farm life forever.

Despite all their hard work and long days, the couple never had been able to get completely out of debt. Bobby often heard them talking in the evenings, wondering if they would ever be able to get all the bills paid. But the war created a demand for plumbers and pipe fitters, so Bunyan decided to leave the farm and join an uncle in the plumbing business in Nashville.

His first job with the firm was an assignment at Camp Campbell Army Base in Kentucky. This was the first of many military construction jobs that kept him traveling all over the eastern United States. Naturally, Bobby and his mother could not go with him to all of these construction sites. However, the construction wages provided more money than the family had ever had before. They were finally able not only to pay off their debts but to buy a house in Cedar Hill—a town about ten miles from Springfield. Bobby and Bessie liked living in town much better than living in the country. The house was neat, clean and comfortable, and they were both glad to leave behind the gloomy old farmhouse with its dust and spider webs and ghosts. Bobby had his own room, and they lived close to the school so that he could walk or ride his bike to school every day. Town living seemed safer to Bobby, and a lot of his fear of the unknown faded away there.

* * *

Bobby's daddy was away from home most of the time. He came for a visit only every month or so, and Bobby soon became aware that his mama was sometimes fearful and often very lonely. One night in their new home in town, when his mama was getting ready for bed, she saw a man standing outside the window looking in, watching her undress. She called the Sheriff and he came over, fired some shots, supposedly at the culprit, but they never did find or identify him.

In Cedar Hill, as in most small towns, everyone knew everyone else's business, so Bobby and his mama figured that everybody knew his daddy was never at home. And they suspected that the Sheriff knew who was peeping in the window. They figured he allowed the man to get away and then warned him not to let it happen again, but they never knew for sure.

After that, Bessie was afraid to sleep in her room alone, so Bobby had to sleep in the room with her. They had an old shotgun they kept propped up beside the bed in case the peeping Tom came back. Manfully, Bobby promised Bessie he would shoot the rascal himself.

"I can't miss with a shotgun, Mama!" he would declare bravely.

Their new home was near the railroad tracks, and a train came through every hour or so. Many tales were told in town of hobos and tramps and all sorts of crooks in transit coming through on the train. Of course the scary tales fueled their fears and imaginations. Old Satan is always wanting to stir things up and steal away any peace and security by putting such frightening thoughts in our heads.

"Listen!" his mama said one night, after Bobby and his mama were in bed with the shotgun propped beside them. "Someone is trying to get in the back door!"

Bobby sat up and, sure enough, there was a loud rattling noise at the back door. Fear gripped him. He began to picture some peeping Tom, some tramp—no, a whole gang of tramps—trying to get into their little house. What would they do to him and his mama? Would they rob them? Beat them? *Kill them?* He was shaking with fear. His mama was shaking with fear. The whole bed was shaking, and they kept hearing that rattling sound at the back door.

Bobby checked the shotgun to make sure it was loaded, then he raised it and pointed it unsteadily at the door. He was so nervous that even if his daddy had walked through the door at that moment, he probably would have shot him dead. Just about that time, a long noisy freight train began passing by the house.

"He'll try to get in while the train is passing, so that we won't hear him break in," Bessie said.

Sure enough, when the train had passed by, the rattling noise had stopped. For a moment all was quiet.

"He's in!" his mama hissed.

They huddled in the middle of the bed, shaking and terrified. This was the worst fear Bobby had experienced since they left the farm, and he did not remember, in that hour of terror, how he had experienced the ever-watchful care of God Himself. All he could think about was the time his mama had told someone that Bobby was the man of the house, now that her husband was gone so much. She had bragged about how Bobby could take care of them, how Bobby could shoot so well. In spite of his fear, Bobby knew that he had to act like a man and protect his mama no matter what.

He began to pray, to ask Jesus for help. He was so scared that he could only say, "Jesus ... Jesus ...." Then the noise started again ... rattle rattle rattle ... at the back door.

Bobby and his mother cowered in terror, but finally, when the noise got no nearer, they mustered enough courage to get out of bed and move slowly and quietly, shotgun at the ready, across the living room to the kitchen where the noise was coming from. Carefully they crept across the rooms, turning on lights as they went. Finally, turning on the kitchen light, they discovered the cause of the noise.

Relief flooded them as they saw a tiny mouse, caught in a trap by only one leg and his tail, rattling around desperately trying to get loose. They sat on the kitchen floor laughing at themselves and praising God for teaching them such a wonderful lesson about the foolishness of surrendering to the power of fear.

What a wonderful lesson about the power of light too. Jesus is the light of the world, and if we only turn His light upon our fear, we will be able to see that whatever we fear is nothing at all in the light of His wonderful love. Looking back on this incident in later years, Bobby always remembered this second great lesson that God taught him on overcoming fear.

* * *

Bobby started school, first grade at Cedar Hill Elementary, in 1937. He was not the best of students. Growing up with mostly poor black children as playmates, Bobby had adopted the grammar of the poor country folk, and was often ridiculed for his pronunciation of some common words—"doe" for "door" or "flo" for "floor," for example. But Bobby loved his black playmates, and he liked the way they talked. He didn't want to change, but he learned that he had to in order to fit in and pass to the next grade. Still, it gave him a bad feeling about school, and he never wanted to do more than get by in his classes.

By the time Bobby was in third grade, he was resigned to never being the best or the first or the most popular or the smartest kid in class. A bad experience that year with an insensitive teacher further hampered his interest in school.

The teacher was young and pretty, and Bobby liked her a lot. There was also a pretty little girl named Betty, a straight-A student, and Bobby liked her even more. He wanted so much for his pretty teacher and for Betty to like him too. He tried so hard to be cute and funny, so he would get their attention.

One day Bobby managed to be standing next to Betty as they worked math problems at the blackboard. The teacher would call out the problem and all the students were supposed to write on the board what she said. All the students did, except Betty. She wrote something else, and because he was paying attention to Betty instead of what the teacher said, Bobby copied what Betty wrote. He knew that whatever she wrote would be right, and so with great confidence, he copied everything she wrote. When they were all sent to their seats, he could see that all the students had written down the same problem—except Betty and, of course, Bobby. The teacher had deliberately asked Betty to write something different to teach Bobby a lesson about the dangers of copying. Then she pointed it out to the class and suggested they all call him "Copy Cat." Bobby, who had only tried to be cute and pay attention to Betty instead of the teacher, now felt wounded, betrayed and humiliated by the very people he most admired.

His heart writhed with the pain of a nine-year-old boy who already felt poor and left out and now had been rejected and shamed before the world. He thought that no one liked him, and he wanted so much for everyone to like him.

The shameful experience of that day was never to be erased. Even as an adult, Bobby could never add so much as a golf score or bowling score without getting nervous about it if anyone was looking over his shoulder.

The teacher did make a lasting impression that day, though she taught a very different lesson from the one she intended.

But God, in His infinite mercy and power, can take even the worst of our personal experiences and use them for good. In Bobby's case, the memory of that shameful humiliation burned into his consciousness and made him forever more caring and compassionate and understanding of boys and girls with their inattentiveness and their "trying to be cute" behaviors. Although the teacher did not know it nor intend it, God used her insensitivity and cruelty to help Bobby grow up to be not a better math student, but a better parent and grandparent. Truly, it is written:

> *All things work together for good to them that love God.* **(Romans 8:28)**

4/ Baptism of Fear

*I*n 1945, when Bobby reached eighth grade, the family moved to Oak Ridge, Tennessee. Bunyan helped to build that huge Army town of 78,000 people in the middle of a quiet valley in the foothills of the Smoky Mountains. So many people came to Oak Ridge that at first there were not enough houses to hold everyone.

Bobby and his family lived in a trailer park along with many other families. They were there to work together in the massive effort, known as the Manhattan Project, to build the first atomic bomb and end the war with Japan. People moved to Oak Ridge from all over the country and even from some foreign countries.

Bobby thought it was a wonderful place. Here everyone was equal, everyone was friendly. Here, he was not the poor little country boy who talked differently from the "town kids." Everyone was accepted on the same level. Everyone was here working together for one purpose—to help the country end the terrible war that had claimed lives from nearly every family. Everyone walked to school or rode buses. Everyone wore galoshes to walk through the awful clay mud that covered the town where the soil was being pushed aside to build houses and where no sidewalks yet existed.

The townspeople sensed they were growing together into a city of great importance. It was a city that played a role in history as the Atomic City of Oak Ridge. Bobby took great pride in being a part of it, and also pride in his daddy's small part in helping to end the war and save the world from Nazi Germany and Imperial Japan.

* * *

The great changes in the world couldn't overshadow the changes Bobby was experiencing personally. One life-changing event happened the first year after Bobby and his family moved to Oak Ridge. A boy named Jake, who lived near them in the trailer park, became one of Bobby's heroes and his closest friend. Jake was good-looking, had a great personality, was good at sports and was very attractive to the girls of the town. Bobby admired all these traits.

Jake's mother and father were "honky-tonkers" like Bobby's mama and daddy. And like them, Jake's parents worked hard all week, spent Saturday night dancing and drinking, then slept late on Sundays. No church, no Sunday school. Jake's parents were also from the Nashville area, and they frequently went home to visit their folks, just as Bobby's parents did. Jake was older and more mature than Bobby, and so he had more freedom. Jake was allowed to drive the family car and go on dates, while Bobby's mama kept him on a tight rein. She never let him stay in Oak Ridge alone, but always made him go with them when they took trips to Springfield to visit the family back home.

Bobby would have rather stayed in Oak Ridge. He enjoyed being with his new friends, because they could think of so many exciting things to do.

One of their favorite pastimes was swimming. Sometimes they would swim in a local creek or go out to Valley View or Big Ridge State Park. They would slip into places that were not open to the public, like the old rock quarries that had filled up with water, some of them more than a hundred feet deep. One weekend near the end of school, when they had all planned to go to Big Ridge to swim, Bobby's parents made a trip home to Springfield.

Jake begged Bobby's parents to let him stay, but they wouldn't hear of it. All Bobby could think about during that trip was how much fun Jake and the gang were having up at Big Ridge.

As soon as they got back to Oak Ridge, he ran to find Jake and hear about the swimming expedition, but there was no one home at Jake's house. Bobby found another buddy at home in his trailer, and that was who gave him the awful news. He told Bobby that his best friend and hero, Jake, had dived off the dam into a non-swimming area and drowned. He was found snagged under a tree root at the bottom of the lake, his neck broken. Jake was only fourteen years old.

Bobby and all his friends were heart-broken, and Jake's parents were devastated. But, once again, God showed that He is able to use even the worst tragedy, the death of a child, for good purpose. In the middle of the rowdy construction trailer camp, Jake's parents began to hold Bible study for the children. They mourned the fact that they had never taught their own son about Jesus, and they wanted to make sure all of Jake's friends knew about Jesus and accepted His salvation by becoming Christians.

A church was organized in the fast-growing town, and Jake's parents invited all the neighborhood children to go with them to the church meetings. Through the influence of their love and their concern, through the message of an eighty-year-old retired preacher, T. G. Davis, and through the working of the Holy Spirit in his heart, Bobby accepted Christ as his personal Saviour during one of the church meetings.

Perhaps partly because Jake's parents wanted it so much, and partly because Jake's death affected their hearts so deeply, about twenty-five young people joined the church that same night and were later baptized. They began attending church regularly, and the tiny new church grew to become the Robertsville Baptist Church of Oak Ridge. Many of the parents of the young people began to attend church, including Bobby's mama and daddy. Bessie later became the first church secretary. Bunyan never learned to love the church as much as he loved playing poker and fishing on Sunday, but Bobby came to know that Jesus loved his daddy, just as He loved everyone else.

For his part, Bunyan Durham, like a lot of other people, found it troubling to see people out sinning all week and then attending church on Sunday. Somehow he felt that attending church should make people perfect like Jesus. Since he knew himself to be considerably less than perfect, his course of reasoning dictated that he stay away from church. He never was able to understand that we are *all* sinners. We sin every day. Only through the overwhelming love and grace of Jesus do any of us ever have deliverance and forgiveness from our sins. God said in His Word to the church:

> *If we say that we have no sin, we deceive ourselves, and the truth is not in us. If we confess our sins, he is faithful and just to forgive us our sins, and to cleanse us from all unrighteousness.* **(I John 1:8-9)**

5/ A New Beginning

Living in Oak Ridge was truly a new beginning, a new life for Bobby. Here no one asked what your daddy did for a living. In Cedar Hill, if you were born on the wrong side of the tracks, you could never cross over. Because Bobby was born to poor farmers who owned nothing, he had developed a terrible feeling of inferiority that the attitudes of those around him in that small town had fed. And because the townspeople looked down on him and his parents, he had believed the town was right, and that he and his family were all somehow less worthy and not as good as others. He thought he was dumber than the children he knew and therefore had never tried to be a good student. He felt clumsier than others and so never had tried to be a good athlete.

Others had laughed at him, at his country way of talking and his country clothes. But because laughter is better than jeers, Bobby had learned how to make them laugh even more. He had become the class clown, always ready with a trick or a joke to make his classmates laugh.

Bessie always encouraged Bobby to study and be a good student. She valued learning and she remembered her school days as some of the happiest days of her life. Bobby never found that to be so, but he wanted to please his mama and he made the best of it.

As Bobby grew up in Oak Ridge High School, he developed more confidence. Being treated as an equal, he came to see himself in a better light. Becoming a Christian helped him to see that he was a precious child of God, loved by God as much as any of His other children.

Along with the new self-esteem came better grades, and Bobby discovered that he even had artistic talent. Combining this with his gift for always seeing the funny side of people and events, he became cartoonist for the high school newspaper. He also developed physically and discovered that his natural coordination gave him an opportunity to excel in sports. He tried out for the football team, the boxing team and got involved in intramural sports.

At the same time, he began to take tentative steps toward paying his way in the world. He worked part-time for the city Recreation Department and as an usher at the Grove movie theater. As if this were not enough, he also took on a newspaper route. Still, he didn't take school classes very seriously and always found time for the activities he enjoyed, such as ogling the girls at the Wildcat Den (a local high school hangout), shooting pool, playing ping-pong, and swimming in the large spring-fed Oak Ridge Pool.

It was at the pool where he really began to pay attention to girls, and there he met his first real girlfriend. Maybe it was because he was so close to his mama that Bobby had always liked girls, appreciated them and admired them. Spurred by his growing confidence and the hormones of a normal male adolescent, Bobby began to date lots of girls in high school. He went steady with three girls in succession. He learned to dance and enjoyed holding the girls close on the dance floor and, later, elsewhere.

He and his girlfriends attended all the school dances, including the junior and senior proms, which were most special. But he enjoyed other activities too. Football games, basketball, track, baseball, swimming and boxing were all fun now that he no longer felt left out and inferior.

Bobby enjoyed church activities, too—parties and games that were good clean fun. He loved the worship services, and he loved learning about Jesus, and how to live and love and respond to family members and others in a loving, Christian way. Church life was new and wonderful to Bobby, and he eagerly drank it in. He had many friends, and he began to think of himself as a lucky person, a person blessed by God.

* * *

After graduating from high school, Bobby entered the nearby University of Tennessee in Knoxville. Because he enjoyed cartooning, he decided to major in commercial art. He hoped to someday have his own cartoon strip. God had given him a wonderful imagination and talent, and he recognized that he could use that talent in a good and creative way. While he liked people, he realized that he also enjoyed being alone with his imagination, creating his own version of the world through his imaginative and humorous cartoon characters.

Although he was learning that he could be good at many things, he never was *best* at anything. And he wanted to be.

Within the imaginary world of his cartoons, he could be the winner, the champion, the hero, and others could be the clowns. As always, he didn't take his class work too seriously, but he always managed to do well enough to get by. Only in his cartooning did he really try to excel. His effort would be rewarded with a life-long skill that would provide a satisfying and rewarding living. That would come later, however, for God had many trials in store for Bobby.

6/ Boot Camp and Other miseries

In 1950, the Korean War began, and Bobby joined the Marines. He did so partly because he was brought up to be patriotic, partly because he wasn't enjoying college very much. Besides, he figured he would be drafted into the Army if he didn't go ahead and volunteer. Later, after his decision had led him to the trenches of Korea, he liked to look back on that decision and say, "See how dumb I was?" Even though God would use Bobby's decision for a good purpose in the world, Bobby couldn't see that at the time.

After all, he was shipping out to Parris Island, South Carolina for boot camp—"Hell on Earth," as he later described it. The Marine Corps made him and a lot of other recruits realize just how nice things had been back home.

Boot camp was a real shock to the system. First the Marines took Bobby's nice clothes, then they shaved his head. This was particularly hard to take, as Bobby's mama always used to say his hair was the prettiest thing about him. They gave him drab uniforms that made him look just like every other miserable recruit, and gave him a number, "just like in prison," he thought, as he cried and longed for home. But he didn't cry alone, and he didn't do badly in boot camp. Aided by his strong young body and his ROTC training at UT, he adapted pretty quickly to the military life. He was about two weeks into boot camp and just becoming comfortable—even a little proud of being a Marine—when the worst tragedy of his life struck hard.

Coming back to Oak Ridge over the Cumberland Mountains from one of their weekend trips to Springfield, his parents had a terrible automobile accident near Rockwood, Tennessee. Bessie and Bunyan both were injured badly and were taken to a local hospital, then later transferred to the Oak Ridge Hospital. Bessie died when a blood clot resulting from the accident lodged in her heart.

Bobby was allowed to come home for the funeral. He was so lost and so lonely knowing that the one person who loved him above all others was gone from the world. Although he loved his daddy, it had always been his mama who reigned in his heart. He missed her bitterly as he stood during the grave-side service. He was to miss her more and more as the years passed by.

"There is not much love in this world," Bobby thought. "Never enough love to fill a hungry heart, and when a mother's unconditional love is gone from the world, it can never be replaced."

But God is gracious and merciful, and He never fails to provide comfort and help whenever our need is greatest. He sent Bobby a helpmate and comforter, a friend from his high school and church who gave him love and care and helped him recover from the grief and mourning for his mama. He needed this girl's compassion and caring, and he grew to love her. He made love to her, and before he returned to the Marines, he married her.

His bride was young and beautiful and kind. She helped him look after Bunyan, who remained in the hospital for a long time recovering from his injuries.

Bobby was his parents' only child, and he tried to get hardship discharge out of the Marines, so that he could care for his father and remain with his wife. The doctors were not sure his daddy would ever be able to walk again, and there was no one else in the family to help him, but the Marine Corps refused to release Bobby. He had to go back to boot camp and begin all over again. Bobby wrote to his Congressman, Howard Baker, Sr., who tried to help. Both Baker and a lawyer Bunyan hired wrote letters to the Marine Corps Commandant asking for his release from the service, but the Marines refused to let him go.

Alhough Bobby saw others with less hardship than his own get a hardship discharge, he was not able to get a release. Finally he gave up and accepted it as the will of God that he should remain in the Marines. Although he couldn't understand it, Bobby read again God's promise that:

> *All things work together for good to them*
> *that love God.* (**Romans 8:28**)

Now more than ever, Bobby turned to the Word of God for comfort and guidance. He began trying to practice what the Bible teaches:

*In everything give thanks: for this is the
will of God in Christ Jesus concerning
you.* (I Thessalonians 5:18)

He stayed in the Marine Corps and, through the
strength gained from God's Holy Word, tried to make the
best of what seemed to be the worst thing that had ever
happened to him. And again God's power was at work,
bringing about good even in the midst of all the pain and
sorrow.

Bunyan stayed in the hospital for eight weeks.
During this time, he was well-cared for, particularly by
one of the special-care nurses.

Emily was a native of Ireland, a World War II bride
brought to this country by her soldier husband. After a
few months, her soldier had abandoned her and their two
beautiful daughters, and she was left to bring them up
alone. Emily worked days and went to school at night.
Taking care of her two baby girls and taking care of
Bunyan, who also needed her, was not easy. Bunyan was
grateful for her friendship and her special attention, and
they became very close. Out of their need for each other
grew love, and they married a few months after Bunyan
left the hospital.

God knows, *always knows*, the needs of our life. He
wants to fulfill those needs and, if we will be open to
receive His blessings, our needs will always be met. "How
gracious and how good is the Lord Our God," thought
Bobby, when he learned of the marriage. Bunyan's wounds
were healed. Not only the physical wounds of his body,
but much more healing was provided for the emotional
and spiritual wounds he had suffered through the loss of

his wife. And by becoming Bunyan's wife, Emily's needs were met also. Bobby's daddy became as good a husband and father as he knew how to be; a good worker and provider, just as he had always been for his family.

Hand grenades hang ready for use beside an automatic rifle, radio and manuals atop an earthen bunker on the Main Line of Resistance in Korea. Outpost Reno, where Bobby's courage would be tested, is the knoll at top, just left of center.

7/ On to Korea

When Bobby finally completed boot camp, he felt he had truly left childhood behind. Now he was Bob the man, the Marine.

He was stationed at Camp Pendleton, near San Clemente, California, for Advanced Infantry Training in preparation for service in Korea.

This was not as bad as boot camp. Now that his father was out of the hospital and well cared for, Bob's bride could come join him in California. It was a happy time for the young couple. Bob later said it was "like going to school, football practice, honeymoon and vacation all rolled into one." The young man and woman enjoyed each other and their life together, always conscious of the war waiting for Bob across the Pacific and aware that this could well be the only time together they would ever share.

They rented a nice apartment near the beach, spent all the money Bob made and borrowed more. His wife liked having money and the pleasures of life that money can buy. Bob enjoyed pleasing his new wife, so they lived it up. There was a sense that there might not be any more time for living, so why not live it up now? Bob went to camp and trained for war all day, then went home and partied and loved his new wife at night. What the heck! Korea was the next stop and he might never see her or America again.

The joyful days ended when orders came for Bob to join many other Marines, most of them young recruits like himself, on a large troop ship headed for the battlefields of Korea. As the ship sailed out of San Diego harbor, Bob stood on deck and watched all that he knew and loved fade slowly from sight. Never had he been so alone. Finally there was nothing but water, water everywhere. The ship seemed small and insignificant, a tiny chip floating on the vast ocean around him. Bob, like many of the other men, wondered if he would ever come home again.

"Oh, God," he prayed, "You have given me a good life. I don't want to die yet. Please let me come back home safe. Please let me come back home and live for You. I will do whatever You want me to do. Please, Lord Jesus, let me live."

He poured all the loneliness and fear and pain of separation from home and loved ones into his prayers. They sailed out, under the vast sky above the tiny ship on the seemingly endless, dark sea.

* * *

For three days after praying earnestly to live, Bob was so sick he wanted to die. He was sicker than he had ever been in his life. For three days and three nights he could keep nothing down, and he felt the overwhelming misery of unending nausea that only seasickness can bring. Quickly he learned not to vomit over the side of the ship, since the wind only blew it back into his face. After the first and only such experience, he carried a bucket with him everywhere. On his fourth day at sea, hunger drove him to the mess hall in spite of his illness. When the man sitting across from him vomited into his tray, Bob quickly forgot the need for food and ran to find his bucket again. On the fifth day, he finally "got his sea legs," and the nausea eased to the point where he could handle a meal. After that he thought of himself as an "Old Salt" and had no more problems with seasickness on the voyage.

Loneliness and fear were still constant companions, however, and many heartfelt prayers and promises were offered up to God during the twenty-one days of the ship's passage.

After a brief stopover in Japan, the ship reached Inchon Bay, South Korea. It arrived on a cold December day, thirty degrees below zero, with snow on the ground and wind blowing fifty miles an hour. It was cold such as the Southern boy had never experienced.

Along with other nervous Marine recruits, he was ordered aboard a train and transported immediately to a camp near the front lines. Unloading from the train, Bob could hear the roar of gunfire not far away. Trucks transported the troops the rest of the way to the front, very near the action. That night the men were assigned to a company and a squad.

Each squad of thirteen men was given a tent with Army bunks and one gas stove for heat. There was no running water, no indoor toilets, no toilet paper. It was easier for Bob than for some of the others to adjust to the crude conditions.

"Just like being back on the farm," he thought, except that, for once, he wished he *were* back on the farm instead of on this snowy, God-forsaken battlefield.

Bob prayed again for life and for the chance to go home to see his wife and father and to have the opportunity to serve God in his own country. Then, in spite of his fatigue, Bob spent a restless first night in Korea listening to the sounds of artillery, mortar and small-arms fire at close range. He was experiencing, first-hand, the fear of battle.

* * *

He surprised himself by adjusting quickly to the hardships of Marine camp life. Bob was young and strong, and the Spirit of God gave him an inner peace and confidence that few of the raw recruits could manage. He thought he was making out pretty well until a day came when he was assigned to an evacuation team.

His company was sent to carry wounded men from the front lines to a rear area where helicopters could pick up the wounded for transport to a hospital ship stationed offshore at Inchon Bay. Bob was given the job of stretcher-bearer. The fields and rice paddies were filled with mines and booby traps, and fraught with barbed wire barriers to force unwary soldiers *into* the mines and booby traps. Everywhere the evacuation team went, they had to move single-file to avoid what would have been instant death from a careless step on a hidden explosive.

This was Bob's first experience working under fire, and he didn't even have a gun. He was nervous, but handled it well at first. Then he saw his first dead body. Then another and another. He looked closer and saw that all of the dead men were Marines. None were the bodies of the enemy.

He grew more and more nervous as his unit continued to move single-file along the path, weaving their way through the rice paddies and the mine fields, with mortar fire and gunfire and explosions all around, as his unit searched among the dead bodies for wounded soldiers who could be carried to safety. He heard for the first time the sounds of bullets flying through the air around him. He knew with heart-freezing certainty that those bullets were aimed at him and his fellow Marines.

Someone called for a stretcher and Bob started running over the frozen ground toward the caller, forgetting the danger of mines and bullets in the urgency of responding to the call for help. His feet slipped on the frozen surface of the rice paddy through which he ran and he fell flat, sliding across the ice on his back. As he lay there for a moment, stunned from the fall, he saw machine gun bullets whizzing over his head, exactly where he had been standing a moment before.

"Thank You for Your deliverance, Lord!" he prayed quickly, and then, as soon as he could, he jumped to his feet and headed for the wounded man.

All through the long, cold, miserable day, he and the other Marines of his company worked like madmen to carry the wounded soldiers back to the helicopter site. He saw men with legs blown away, men missing arms and eyes, strong men covered with blood, moaning and crying in agony. He saw men with holes blown through their flesh by mines or mortar fire, bullets and mine fragments sticking from the flesh, and he saw so many who were dying or already dead.

It was the most horrible day of his life. Finally it was over, and, with his company of dog-tired Marines, he made it back to the cold tent and the indescribable comfort of a warm sleeping bag.

8/ A Personal Armageddon

*B*ob was not assigned to any more evacuation duty, and he thanked God for that. Instead, his company was stationed on the Main Line of Resistance (MLR), a battle trench dug all the way across the countryside of Korea. The United Nations armed forces had been deployed to maintain this line of resistance to protect South Korea from the invasion of North Korean Communist troops.

The forces of each United Nations participant were given a section to maintain. Bob, like most of the other Marines, didn't even know which countries were assisting with other sections of the MLR; they only knew what their responsibility was, and they knew they might be asked to die to carry out their mission.

The MLR trench was dug four to twelve feet deep, with bunkers located about every twenty or thirty feet. These bunkers were manned twenty-four hours a day. The

Marines standing guard duty continued to dig out the trench and worked to repair the bunkers and sections of the trench that were damaged by nightly mortar attacks.

The countryside was raw and battered from the mortar fire. It was a desolate land, and the snow and ice and wind added to the misery of every task. Bob looked at the area with the eyes of a farmer and decided it was a poor country, not good for anything much except for growing rice. Some of the area around the MLR looked remotely like some of the poorer sections of Tennessee, although the trees and bushes were smaller and scrappier. There were small, rolling hills and a few high hills that reminded him of the Smoky Mountain foothills or the Cumberlands so far away.

* * *

Bob soon learned that the high hills were key observation points. Many of the fiercest battles were fought for possession of the high ground. Three hills in particular, located two or three miles north of the MLR in what was called "no man's land," were frequented by patrols of the North Korean troops and by U.S. Marine patrols as well. Sometimes there were skirmishes or "fire fights" between these roaming patrol bands. The U.S. troops gave the three hills the code names Reno, Vegas and Carson to keep enemy troops from knowing exactly where the patrols were located should radio messages be intercepted.

Reno was the highest of the hills, and therefore the most valuable observation post. It was constantly guarded by both enemy and U.S. troops. Three squadrons of U.S. forces at a time were given two-week patrol duty assignments in the trenches surrounding Reno before being relieved by another group of forty-two men. There was a cave dug into the side of the hill where the men slept and rested during breaks from guard duty. The only safe path to Reno was a trail winding through the rice paddies leading from the MLR to the base at Reno. Soldiers kept to the path to avoid the mine fields, and each night a thirteen-man patrol was sent out to keep the path clear of mines and booby traps.

Since the base camp was always under close enemy observation, almost all activity was carried out at night. During the day, the Marines slept or stood watch or dug, deepening the trenches and the hillside cave.

Bob has said he lived like a mole, always underground in caves, bunkers, holes, or sometimes in a small pup tent pitched in the deepest part of the trench. At the Reno outpost, the only food was "C-rations" (canned beans, canned hamburger, canned Spam, or canned chicken). Occasionally the men were allowed to heat the rations on a small gas stove or with canned heat, but the food quickly cooled again in the windy cold of the trench.

An enemy soldier was captured one night by Bob's patrol squad. From him the Americans learned that enemy troops had been given orders to capture all the high ground before the spring thaw turned the surrounding frozen ground into a sea of mud. U.S. troops were already aware of the unusual activity that began around Reno in the month of March. Not long after the enemy soldier was captured, Bob's squadron was relieved at Reno and went back to their duty at the MLR.

* * *

One night the gates of hell seemed to open up and swallow the world in everlasting fire. To Bob, it seemed the End of Time was at hand. The sky was as bright as day and nothing could be heard but the booming and screaming fire of mortars, artillery and air strikes. Bullets thundered and hissed through the air above the MLR. All the fireworks of a hundred Fourth of July celebrations and all the fears of a lifetime came together at once in that terrifying night. Bob was so afraid he couldn't even bring himself to look out of the trench. He huddled into the deepest curves of the dirt wall that he could find, praying and reading his Bible in that awful flashing light of the battle fire. Suddenly, he heard the sergeant call his name.

"Get your gear! We're moving out to back up Reno! They're being overrun."

Bob knew a lot of the men out there in the middle of that hell at the Reno base, and he instantly thought of how it would feel to be there, right in the center of the screaming Armageddon of artillery fire. He didn't hesitate.

"With God's help, we'll get them out," was his only thought, as he quickly gathered his gear and joined his buddies on the run.

9/ Faith Under Fire

Leaving the protection of the MLR trench and heading into the ferocious battle fire of "no-man's land" was one of the hardest things Bob had ever done, but he did it as any well-trained Marine would, quickly and efficiently. And he did it as any Christian brother would, going without hesitation to help his comrades in their hour of greatest danger. The soldiers ran through the gate into no-man's land one at a time, watching the trail for recently placed booby traps, and fighting their way through the enemy ambushes set up along the way.

The enemy had zeroed in on the well-used trail. Mortar shells were hitting about five feet apart, and bombs were exploding on all sides. Bob felt like a human target, totally exposed and vulnerable. But the words he had learned in his youth, the words of the Lord God of Hosts, stayed within his mind and gave him the courage to keep running forward into that awful world of death.

The Lord is my light and my salvation;
whom shall I fear? the Lord is the strength
of my life; of whom shall I be afraid?
When the wicked, even mine enemies and
my foes, came upon me to eat up my flesh,
they stumbled and fell. (Psalm 27:1-2)

About fifty Marines left the MLR in front of Bob, heading for the U.S. trenches leading to the top of Reno. By the time he reached those trenches, Bob was the lead man, because so many brave men had fallen along the way. So many lives already were lost in that hellish world of fire and smoke and deadly missiles. The enemy had the remaining U.S. troops pinned down. There was no way to move forward to the top of Reno, since the North Korean troops had taken over the U.S. positions there. Attempts to advance with ground troops would have been suicidal.

The Marines were desperately trying to hold their position when word came down the line from the commanding officers to pull back down the hill into a safer area. There were so many wounded and dead all around. The knee-deep trench was soaked in blood, and everywhere were men, torn and bleeding, moaning and crying, or ripped into pieces and not moving at all. Bob had been the first man into the trenches and, since the Marines had to withdraw in single file to stay within the meager cover of the knee-deep trench, he would have to be the last to leave.

Just as he started to obey the order and follow the others back down the hill, one of his wounded buddies lying at his feet reached out and grabbed his leg.

"Please don't leave us! We'll all be killed." Bob looked down into the begging eyes of a blood-soaked Marine.

He wanted to go. He had orders to go. Every muscle, nerve, and tendon was poised to escape this death trap. He was more afraid than he had ever been in his life. He didn't want to die. He especially didn't want to be wounded and crippled for the rest of his life. But the power of the Holy Spirit—that Power and Shield of Faith that had been within his heart since childhood to help overcome his fear—was strong within him now. Bob decided instantly that he had to stay where he was and defend his brothers. He prayed more earnestly than he had ever prayed that God would help him get the wounded men back down the hill to safety. Again the words of God came to his mind and heart, and again they gave him strength to stand.

> *The Lord is my light and my salvation; whom shall I fear?* (**Psalm 27:1**)

Bob stayed where he was, and the fear in his heart was conquered. He sent word back up the line to the commanding officer that he was going to stay in place until all the wounded could be moved out. He asked for more ammo for his Browning automatic rifle and requested reinforcements be sent to help carry out the wounded.

And then, to draw the enemy fire from his retreating buddies and his wounded companions, Bob stood up alone in the knee-high trench and fired his Browning into the maelstrom of battle that surrounded him. He could see no individual enemy faces—only the silhouettes of men running through the smoke and light of the explosives landing a few hundred feet from the trench or sometimes in the trench only yards away from where he stood. The Browning was heavy, and it was impossible to aim at any specific target in that fire storm of battle. He realized he was the only man left in the trenches able to stand, and his was the only workable weapon left there; so he simply held the Browning at his hip and fired toward the dark enemy silhouettes until the rifle barrel was white hot. The Lord God of Hosts stood with him, shielded him and gave him the strength to withstand the enemy alone. The enemy stumbled and fell.

* * *

After what seemed an endlessly long time, reinforcements came, and all of the wounded Marines were moved out to safety down the hill. Of the twenty-seven men in Bob's unit who went up Reno, twenty were killed and six were wounded. Only Bob came out of that battle untouched.

Thinking later of the miraculous experience of that night, when angels surely surrounded and protected him from the heavy enemy fire, Bob wondered how many people at home were praying for him and with him that night. Perhaps his wife and his father and stepmother were on their knees in prayer for him. Maybe his pastor and some faithful members of his church back in Oak Ridge also prayed for him and other soldiers on frozen Korean battlefields. He thought of his praying friends and family with gratitude and longing. But he knew with absolute certainty that God had heard and answered his own earnest prayers in that trench.

Although Bob received acclaim from everyone there for his outstanding bravery, he knew the truth. Without the strength of the Holy Spirit, he surely would have run from that bloody and dangerous trench. He knew that the Almighty God of all creation had shielded him from all harm; had preserved his life and the lives of his wounded buddies for a purpose. He knew that God is not only the author and creator of all life, but of each *individual* life, including his own life.

The absolute certainty of that truth filled him with wonder. He began spending more time reading his Bible, trying to discover the reason God might want Bob Durham, an ordinary country boy from Tennessee, to remain alive in the world when so many had died. One passage of scripture, especially, spoke to him.

> *Go home to thy friends, and tell them how great things the Lord hath done for thee, and hath had compassion on thee.*
> **(Mark 5:19)**

"Yes!" Bob said, when he read that passage, "Yes, Lord, I will tell them how wonderful *You* are. How merciful and good *You* are. I know it wasn't Bob who stood up to the enemy; I know it was *You*."

But the Marine Corps gave Bob all the credit for his bravery. He was nominated by his peers to receive the Silver Star Medal, the third-highest award given by the U.S. Marine Corps for valor in action. Bob was declared a hero by his comrades, and he was pleased and proud to be seen in this light by his fellow Marines.

He tried to tell everyone that it was the Spirit of God that empowered him to act bravely even when his heart was full of fear. He testified to anyone who would listen that God's scriptures are true, and that His Word lives through us when we have faith and believe.

Because of his relatively Puritanical standards, his constant Bible study, and his habit of "looking after" those who needed help, Bob had already been given the nickname of "Maw" by his squad. He didn't really mind the name, since it was given with affection. He enjoyed having the friendship and respect of his fellow Marines, even though he constantly told the men that it was Jesus who really cared about them, while he, Bob, didn't really "give a damn" about them. But, of course, he loved them all, and his proudest moments came when some of his friends, including his special buddy, Griff, accepted Jesus Christ as Lord, at least partly because of his testimony to God's grace and goodness.

* * *

After the terror and excitement of this battle at Reno, the squadron and the whole company had lost so many men that an almost completely new group of replacements were sent in. The new squad leader and most of the new

Marines had never been in any action before. Everything was different with all the old guys gone, especially when the company was sent to the rear for rest and recreation.

When "Charlie Company" (Company C, First Battalion, Fifth Marines) was voted the most outstanding company on the whole Main Line of Resistance, there was a big celebration with lots of cold beer, good food and good music. The men joked and partied and drank, trying this one night to forget the ones who had died, the brave Marines no longer among them. As the hero of the hour, Bob was caught up in the celebration. For the first time in his life, he drank too much and got really drunk and really sick.

Everyone in the squadron drank too much. A fight broke out in the tent, and in the melee every bunk was turned over, every mosquito net torn down, except the squadron leader's. He was new and mean and tough, and everyone was afraid to bother his stuff. When Bob came staggering into the tent and saw that his own bunk and everyone else's was messed up and only the squadron leader's left intact, he took a flying leap through the air into the leader's bunk, tearing down the mosquito netting and going right out through the wall of the tent into the yard's mud and gravel. This pretty well broke up the party. His buddies got him up and cleaned him off, took off all his clothes and painted Mercurochrome on the scrapes and scratches all over his body. Bob looked like he had been stabbed or in a fight with a wildcat. Still partially drunk, he scraped off his bunk, lay down naked and immediately fell asleep.

Sometime later Bob woke up with his first hangover. His head felt swollen big as a pumpkin. Pain such as he had never known filled it from ear to ear, from eyeball to eyeball. Still woozy and a little drunk, he realized he had to go to the toilet, about fifty yards from the tent. Forgetting that he was still naked, Bob grabbed his helmet (a good Marine never goes outside without his helmet) and headed for the latrine. About halfway there, he came face to face with the Company Commander. Suddenly realizing that he was not only drunk but naked and definitely out of uniform, Bob braced himself for a royal Marine "chewing out," but he didn't know what to do except salute. The Commander just smiled and returned his salute, as they posted past one another in the dark.

Private First Class Robert S. Durham, front row, third from right (and third to the right of the American flag), stands at attention during ceremonies in which he received the Silver Star for valor during combat.

Lab Member's Son Wins Silver Star

Robert S. Durham

America's third highest award for valor in action will soon be bestowed upon a 21-year-old Oak Ridge Marine hero, Robert S. Durham, the son of Bunyon Durham, a member of Oak Ridge National Laboratory's Engineering and Maintenance Division.

In a letter to his father, dated June 9, Robert told him of the encounter with the enemy on Reno Hill, a North Korean outpost; and very modestly related that he had been recommended for the Silver Star for staying with his wounded buddies until reinforcements arrived.

The Oak Ridger is a member of Charlie Company of the Fifth Marines in Korea, ordered to move up on Reno to retake the vital hill. After fighting through a Chinese ambush, Charlie Company, with casualties already heavy, moved into striking distance of the objective. While waiting for reinforcements, the enemy began moving in on the Company, taking a heavy toll of the Marine outfit.

Surrounded by wounded buddies, Durham singlehandedly held off attacking troops with a Browning automatic until the reinforcements arrived.

Durham cautioned his father about "saying anything about my decoration." It was only after an Associated Press wire story related the feats of Durham and his buddies that persons outside the family knew of the decoration. The Oak Ridger was the only member of the company not killed or wounded in the bloody battle.

This story appeared on July 17, 1953 in *The Oak Ridge National Laboratory News,* published by Bunyan Durham's employer. The newspaper announced that Bob would receive the Silver Star.

The President of the United States takes pleasure in presenting the SILVER STAR MEDAL to

PRIVATE FIRST CLASS ROBERT S. DURHAM,
UNITED STATES MARINE CORPS,

for service as set forth in the following

CITATION:

"For conspicuous gallantry and intrepidity while serving as an Automatic Rifleman of Company C, First Battalion, Fifth Marines, First Marine Division (Reinforced), in action against enemy aggressor forces in Korea on 26-27 March 1953. When the company was subjected to intense hostile small-arms, mortar and artillery fire while advancing in a counterattack against a vital enemy-held outpost, Private First Class Durham was the first man to reach the intermediate objective and, when the enemy charged under cover of the barrage, courageously stood up, exposing himself to the hostile fire to bring devastating counterfire to bear on them which accounted for many enemy dead and wounded. With the action becoming more intense, he fearlessly continued to expose himself to the hostile fire, delivering accurate fire and hurling grenades and, when ordered to withdraw, took up a position at the rear of his unit to cover the evacuation of the many casualties. By his gallant fighting spirit, daring initiative and unswerving devotion to duty, Private First Class Durham served to inspire all who observed him and upheld the highest traditions of the United States Naval Service."

For the President,

C. S. Thomas
Secretary of the Navy.

This citation, bearing the signature of Navy Secretary C.S. Thomas, accompanied the Silver Star Medal given to Pvt. 1st Class Robert S. Durham, an automatic rifleman of Company C ("Charlie Company"), First Battalion, Fifth Marines, First Marine Division. He was awarded the honor for the courage he displayed during battle at Outpost Reno near the Main Line of Resistance in Korea, March 26-27, 1953.

A relaxed Bob Durham poses for a picture during a period of rest and relaxation.

Bob and Margaret Durham, above, in a photograph taken in 1989.
Below, Bob looks at faces of dead soldiers gazing from a wall of
the Korean War Memorial at dedication ceremonies in July 1995.

10/ Rest and Recreation

During this period of R&R, Bob loved being able to go to church, where he would ask forgiveness for some of his foolish behaviors. He really enjoyed the fellowship with other Christians, but he also became involved in lots of other things. These included athletic activities he had been good at in high school, such as football and boxing. There were other activities unique to the military, like the drill team. He also volunteered to do some graphic arts work—painting signs for all the squad tents. He would do almost anything to get out of the nasty and boring chores, such as mess duty, digging trenches and latrines, and playing war games, and his ability as an artist came in handy.

These were good, relaxed times. At age twenty-one, Bob was now a little older than many of the new recruits. Most of the men were eighteen to twenty. Despite their efforts to make him a hero, Bob pointed out that at the time of his heroic behavior he had been, in fact, as terrified as the next guy, and only Jesus gave him the power to act with bravery. He retained a deep and sincere consciousness of his own weaknesses and failures, so he never developed the "holier-than-thou" attitude that so many religious folks exhibit. He was a "regular guy," a "man's man," but he didn't hesitate to let everyone know that, although he was a miserable sinful Marine like all the rest of them, his Savior, Jesus, was perfect. Bob never tired of telling them this truth, often in language they would most readily understand.

"Jesus understands and loves me just the way I am," he would say, adding in the jocular, Marine way of talking, "And He loves *you too*, you miserable S.O.B.!"

He never missed an opportunity to share the Good News about Jesus Christ and His redeeming love. Whether in the barracks, the battlefield or, sometimes, even in the bar, he encouraged these raw young recruits to read their Bibles, to go to church, chapel, or mass, to stay out of trouble and to thank God for all the blessings of life. He continued to be "Maw" to those he thought of as "his boys."

* * *

One of the highlights of this R&R period for Bob was being able to play football with a lot of good college players. Although he had always wanted to be a team star in high school, he had matured more slowly than some of his classmates and never was able to make the first team.

With all the fitness training of the Marine Corps, and with the additional size, strength and confidence that came through maturity, Bob was now able to play with the best of them.

His good friend, Griff, for instance, had played football for the University of Florida. Griff was the first person Bob had met in Korea. On their first evening, standing in line waiting to wash their mess gear, Bob had heard Griff singing lines from an old country music song, "Way down in Columbus Georgia ... How I long to be back in Tennessee." This really struck a familiar chord in the homesick Bob, and he spoke up.

"I sure would like to be back in Tennessee tonight, too," he said.

From that beginning they discovered they were both displaced Southern boys, both loved football, and both even knew a lot of the same players on the Florida and Tennessee teams. They soon had become good buddies and especially enjoyed arguing about the Southeastern Conference teams. Griff was the one who started calling Bob "Maw." He was with Bob in the battle at Outpost Reno, and he received a wound there that kept him away from the squad for a while.

During the R&R period, Griff recovered enough to be sent back to the unit, and Bob was really glad to see him whole again. One Sunday afternoon Griff came over to talk to Bob.

"Maw," he said, "I accepted Jesus as my personal Saviour today."

"That's great, Griff! I'm really happy for you."

"Do you know why I did that?" Griff asked.

"No, I don't," Bob admitted.

"Well, it's because of the way that you used the Word of God to overcome your fear on the battlefield at Reno. You kept talking about Jesus being our Saviour—how He wants to save us from all fear, sickness, death and anything that is not heavenly. And it's the way you always volunteer to go out on patrol when nobody else is willing to do it. I got to thinking. How can you do that night after night? Facing death, or the possibility of being crippled for life, maybe losing an arm or a leg. And you always laughed and said 'I'm a Tennessee Volunteer and, besides, Jesus is my Saviour. He saves me now, just the same as He saved His disciples back when the Good Book was written.' And you would always open the Bible and show me where it is written:

But as many as received him, to them gave he power to become the sons of God. (John 1:12)

"And," Griff added, "You'd always laugh and say, 'I really believe that stuff.' So that, finally, I've come to believe it too."

This conversion and testimony of his friend, Griff, affected Bob more deeply and pleased him more, even, than receiving the Silver Star. After that, he and Griff frequently talked about how the power of God could help even the weakest to stand firm and strong in battle, while they personally saw many big strong Marines, powerful athletes and well-trained fighting men become so terrified that they would freeze. Some would have to have their weapons pried from their hands so that other soldiers could use them. They would cry like babies and were pitiful to see, both on the battlefield and afterward, when they were overcome with shame for their cowardice.

Yet Bob understood exactly how they felt. He had been overcome with fear himself, both as a small boy terrified of unknown sounds and shadows in his own house and yard and, not long ago, as a soldier facing known enemies on the battlefield. As a boy, he had been given the revelation that guardian angels surrounded him, shielding him with God's protective love, no matter what dangers might come. As a man, he again had experienced that protective, caring love of God that shielded him from all harm, even in a fire storm of bullets and exploding bombshells. He had learned, from reading the Word of God, that our heavenly Father does not want his children to be afraid. He commands us to "Fear not!" God wants us to trust Him to care for us in all circumstances of life, no matter how dangerous, tedious, or difficult

So then faith cometh by hearing, and hearing by the word of God. **(Romans 10:17)**

And when we *do* trust Him, He *does* provide for us wonderfully, miraculously, beyond even our wildest dreams. Bob had learned the truth of this gospel message through his own life's experiences. He knew that he would continue throughout his life to learn more about the shielding, protecting power of faith in God. And he knew that through faith came freedom from fear.

This blurred phtograph, taken by a fellow Marine, shows Bob, at left, delivering a left jab just after his opponent follows through with a right cross. Bob successfully represented "Charlie Company" during competition.

11/ Lord of the Ring

*O*ne of the activities designed to keep the Marines both entertained and in top physical form during their R&R reserve period was a boxing tournament. Now that Bob had the "tough fighting man" reputation among his fellow Marines, they began urging him to enter the tournament to represent them. Bob had lettered in boxing in high school, and had sometimes worked out with a Golden Gloves champion at the Oak Ridge police gymnasium. Backed by his modest experience and the encouragement of his buddies, Bob decided to enter the tournament.

The boxers never knew until a drawing was held who they would be matched up with to fight, or how good their opponents might be. Bob lucked out in his first fight, drawing an opponent who was a boxing novice.

"The guy was so bad," Bob said later, "that he really made me look good." As a result, Bob became one of the company commander's favorites, and all the officers and men placed bets on him to win the tournament. He did go on to win the company championship and then suddenly realized that this meant he had to fight for the battalion championship.

In the first fight at the battalion level, Company C's best man was beaten so badly his eyes were swollen closed and his nose was broken. He was left in such bad shape that he was unable to fight again. The men found out later that his opponent had been a professional fighter in New York City. In these rough-and-tumble Marine matches, nobody really cared much whether the fighters got hurt or how badly. Macho Marines were expected to take the punishment. Although they had referees and followed regular boxing rules during the matches, sometimes these turned into free-for-alls with lax enforcement and a raucous ringside atmosphere.

* * *

The Marines really enjoyed the fights, and big crowds gathered for all the matches. After Company's C's best boxer was defeated, Bob realized it was up to him to represent the men. Despite all his teaching and preaching about overcoming fear, Bob became nervous and afraid. He talked to his coach and let him know that if he ever got in the ring with somebody who was really hurting him badly, he intended to throw in the towel—quit, get out of the ring! The coach said he understood.

But Bob won his next two fights and then was up for the battalion championship match against a really good fighter. Everyone was super-excited about it, talking about how his opponent, the same New York professional who had beaten Company C's best man, had fought more than one hundred matches and won them all! The guy even dressed like a real professional, with his own monogrammed boxing shorts and shoes, and a genuine boxing robe with his name embroidered on it. The outfit alone was enough to intimidate an amateur opponent.

Poor Bob from Tennessee had nothing to wear but Marine-issue khaki shorts, khaki socks, khaki high-top tennis shoes and no robe at all. Some of his best friends asked him to forfeit the match, because they were so afraid he'd really get hurt. Bob actually wanted to quit, but a lot of his officers and men were counting on him, so he decided to go ahead and give it a try, even though he had little hope of winning.

One day prior to the match, Bob walked over to the professional fighter's training ring. Casually walking in, he sat down next to some fellow Marine to watch his opponent work out.

"Gosh, that guy sure looks good," Bob said.

"He is good," the Marine replied.

"Boy, he looks like he doesn't have any weaknesses," Bob continued. He wasn't just making conversation. The boxer was beautiful—fast, muscular, in top condition. Bob thought to himself, *That guy probably even has muscles in his eyebrows.* The man was known to be a hard hitter and had won most of his fights by knockouts.

The Marine sitting next to Bob smiled and said, "I've worked out with him a lot, and he really hits hard, but he does have one weakness. He won't fight inside. He only fights at long range, and all his power is in long looping swings or punches."

Ah, Bob thought, *I'm short, stocky, and I'm best at inside fighting.* Bob walked away from the training ring a little less fearful. He had his game plan.

* * *

On the night of the big championship match, Bob's opponent came by and asked if it was O.K. for them to use professional-style, eight-ounce gloves, rather than the amateur sixteen-ounce gloves that everyone else used. Bob thought it over and decided the boxer really wanted to knock him out or hurt him pretty badly by using the prototype gloves, so he let him know that he intended to use the sixteen-ounce gloves like everyone else.

His opponent got really mad about it—fussed, cussed and fumed—but Bob held firm, and they used the sixteen-ounce gloves. When the bell rang for Round One, Bob put his game plan into action. He got in close and stayed so close that his opponent was unable to use his powerful long swings and punches. Bob grabbed him and held on every chance he got, until the referee would break them up and make both step back. Before his opponent could get off a long, looping punch, Bob would grab him again. He'd also get in a good quick punch going in and a punch coming out.

Before long, the professional fighter was so frustrated he didn't know what to do. He was as mad as a bull, but as soon as he tried to pull back for a long, sweeping punch, Bob, smaller and more agile, would rush toward him, landing a hard body shot on the way in. The crowd was delighted. All of Bob's officers and buddies were yelling and cheering for him, and, with their instinctive impulse to support the underdog, many others in the crowd cheered for him too. A couple of times the professional fighter connected with his sweeping punches, leaving Bob feeling dazed, but he kept on trying.

Once Bob connected with an uppercut square to the chin, and he thought surely the other fighter would go down. But the referee gave him a standing-eight count. This made the professional fighter madder than ever. At one point the referee had to stop the fight to put one of the professional's gloves back on. Bob's elbowing to get the inside position had loosened it. As Bob began to smell victory, he was all over his opponent, "like a chicken on a June bug," as he later described it to his Southern buddies.

The frustrated and befuddled professional never had a chance to fight his own fight. Bob carried out his strategy of "stay inside, stay close" so well that his opponent got few opportunities to show off his boxing skills with long powerful swings and punches. Finally, to the delight of the crowd of Marines, Bob was declared the winner of the match by a unanimous decision of the judges.

Bob, his buddies, and all of "Charlie Company" were deliriously happy that this twenty-to-one underdog amateur had beaten the big, professional fighter. Bob was both amazed and thrilled at winning this second boxing championship. It was unbelievable to him that he—a country boy so afraid he had planned in advance to give up the fight if he started getting hurt—had been made a champion again. He remembered the Bible's account of God giving David the victory over Goliath, and he realized that only God could have given him the victory in this fight too. Before entering the ring, Bob had prayed, asking God to be with him and help him to do his best. He had read the scripture that applied.

> *The lot is cast into the lap; but the whole disposing thereof is of the Lord.* **(Proverbs 16:33)**

Once more, Bob knew that the real source of victory lay in the power of God, not in the skill of Bob. And he let that be known to all who rushed in to congratulate him on his victory.

Bob never boxed again after that. His company commander wanted him to join a team of boxing champions from the First Marine Division that was being organized to fly to Japan to fight against a similar Navy championship team. Bob thought about it. This was a great honor, but he turned it down. He really wanted to stay with his friends and share whatever was coming in the months ahead with them. He enjoyed the admiration of his friends and felt that he no longer had anything to prove. His commanding officer paid him a compliment, telling Bob he was proud to have him in his command. He said Bob upheld the highest traditions of the U.S. Marine Corps and was an inspiration to everyone who knew him.

For the first time in his life, buoyed by such praise, Bob really felt good about who he was, where he was and what he was doing with his life. And he knew he owed it all to God. His always loving and caring Father was watching and guarding him and blessing him here in the middle of this awful war on foreign ground, just as tenderly and carefully as he had watched and guarded and cared for him back home in the green hills of Tennessee.

Bob paints a sign for officers. His ability as a graphic artist allowed him to avoid some of the less glamorous duties of Marine life.

12/ The Hills of Home

*B*ob's best friend, Griff, was shipped back to the U.S. ahead of Bob, and it really left a gap in Bob's life. They had become very close, and each of them had grown in Christian fellowship with one another.

But just after Griff left, God sent another special person into Bob's life. McInturff, from Erwin, Tennessee, arrived in Korea and was assigned to Bob's squad. He was a big, tough former University of Tennessee football player, standing over six feet tall and weighing 275 pounds. Bob admired him and liked him instantly, and the feeling was mutual. They felt almost like family, because they were both from Tennessee, far from home in a sea of strangers. They had a great old time talking about Tennessee home cooking, high school, football, hunting, fishing and their families. They both knew a lot of the same great players at U.T. and never tired of talking about some of the famous plays and games and coaches of the Volunteers.

By this time, Bob had become a legend to the new kids—those raw recruits still being shipped into Korea to join his company. Bob was respected and admired as a seasoned combat veteran, winner of the Silver Star, a champion boxer, and also as the best arm wrestler in the squadron. Or maybe, so the talk went among the guys, maybe he was the best arm wrestler in the Marine Corps. Maybe the best in the whole wide world!

Bob knew that things were getting out of hand with the guys talking about what a "legend" he had become. On the other hand, while he didn't believe it himself—he knew the truth—he still enjoyed the reputation.

After McInturff joined the squad, everyone began promoting the idea of an arm-wrestling contest between McInturff and Durham. Knowing how big and strong McInturff really was, Bob stalled as long as he could, until the contest could be avoided no longer.

Against McInturff's six-feet-two-inch, 275-pound frame, Bob was five-feet-ten and weighed 210. He was aware that McInturff's arms were bigger than Bob's own legs. But he had no choice and, he thought, no chance to win. There was no way he could beat "The Turff," and, realistically, no one else expected him to win either. But everyone likes to see a champion taken down, and, in a way, they all sort of wanted to see the legend get beat.

Looking back, Bob realized he had been pretty obnoxious for some time. He had never been a winner before, but suddenly, within a few months, he had been a winner at everything he tried. It was heady stuff, being a winner and a legend among a bunch of tough Marines. Although he realized the glory all belonged to God, he also had thoroughly enjoyed being the hero for once in his life. And he suspected that he had never kept his mouth shut about it. So he didn't blame the guys for their avid interest in seeing him thoroughly humiliated in an arm-wrestling contest with McInturff.

Finally the appointed day came. The crowd gathered around a table in the mess tent, and the contest started. McInturff was strong as a bull, and Bob soon began sweating profusely. He knew he didn't have a chance, but he was straining so hard the muscles in his arm were trembling. McInturff's arm was steady as a rock. Bob's arm started down in defeat. Bob grimaced, and McInturff grinned. Bob grimaced again. He was almost ready to give up when all at once his arm started to come to life again. After what seemed like hours, the two men came back to a dead-even heat, and neither arm gave a fraction of an inch.

After what seemed more hours, Bob said, "It looks like a draw. Do you want to call it a draw?"

McInturff said, "It's a draw."

Bob thought his arm would never be normal again. He later claimed he couldn't even write his name for about a week, but at the time, he didn't let on. He bragged on how strong McInturff was, and he managed never to arm wrestle again during the whole time he was in Korea.

Anytime anybody wanted to wrestle, he would always say, "If you can beat McInturff, I'll wrestle you." He never had to wrestle again, because McInturff was the strongest human being any of them had ever met. Nobody ever beat him, and nobody else ever even tied him.

No one except McInturff and Bob ever knew the full truth about the arm wrestling match between the two friends, but in talking about it later, Bob would always say, "Thank God for good friends and a buddy who doesn't have to win to prove who's the strongest."

* * *

By this time, a truce had been signed in "the Korean Conflict," as it was then called. The war was never officially won or lost, and only later was it even dignified by the name "The Korean War." The military action there ended in an uneasy cease-fire built around the notion of establishing a two-and-one-half mile wide "demilitarized zone" stretching between North and South Korea, with more than a million troops remaining stationed on each side. Even now, forty-five years later, peace has not been achieved between North and South Korea.

Bob, along with thousands of other Korean War soldiers and their families and friends on both sides of the conflict, was left to wonder what was really accomplished and why so many gave their lives in a war that settled nothing and that ended with an uncertain armistice rather than a lasting peace. But, as always in the course of human history, God was able to use even the greatest evil that Satan can devise—war—for a good purpose in the lives of His people.

Bob had never wanted to go to war in Korea; he had tried as hard as he could to get out of it and stay home to take care of his father and then his own wife who needed him. Like all the other soldiers, he rejoiced when word came that an armistice was signed and they could all go home. Like them, he realized that, painful as his experiences had been, many good lessons had been learned through those tough times.

Bob had learned to rely completely on God, and he had learned beyond all doubt that God will not fail those who place their trust and their lives totally in His care.

During the long journey home to the States, he spent a lot of time thanking God for the lessons of those fourteen months in Korea. No matter what the politicians might do, Bob knew that he and his fellow Marines had done a good job. He thanked God for allowing him to serve his country and his Lord in the U.S. Marine Corps and for helping him to serve honorably. He thanked God that He never asks us to do anything that He will not then enable us to carry through, no matter how small our own strength and abilities. He especially thanked God for family and friends and a free country to call home.

Bob remembered how he had prayed on the ship, when coming to Korea. He remembered how he had asked God to let him live and had promised to dedicate his life in service to God, if only God would protect him through the war.

Now he offered up his heartfelt gratitude to God for answering those prayers and for blessing him in every way. Bob asked God to lend him strength and courage to be faithful to fulfill his own promise. He knew beyond doubt that all of life is given by God and that, in God's master plan, each life has meaning and purpose. Bob knew he had been preserved through all the battles without even a wound, while many others died all around him, because God had some special purpose for his life. He realized as never before how special, how precious, every human life is to our heavenly Father. He humbly recognized that God had preserved him, a poor country boy from Tennessee, and he knew that God would continue to bless him so that he could live out His will. These were the thoughts and prayers in Bob's mind and heart as he sailed home from the Korean War in 1954.

Now unto him that is able to do exceeding abundantly above all that we ask or think, according to the power that worketh in us, Unto him be glory in the church by Christ Jesus throughout all ages, world without end. Amen. **(Ephesians 3:20-21)**

* * *

Bob was given a hero's welcome by his wife, his family and his whole home town. He got a job as a graphic artist back home in Oak Ridge, Tennessee, working for Union Carbide, the contractor organization operating the Oak Ridge National Laboratory. The local newspaper, *The Oak Ridger,* ran an article entitled, "Marine Hero Begins Work in Graphic Arts."

The Lord provided many opportunities for Bob to tell his stories of God's protecting grace on the battlefield, and he shared his experiences freely. He loved witnessing to churches, youth camps, retreats, sports banquets and anywhere else anyone gave him the chance to talk about the Good News and the glory of God's gracious mercy to a fearful Marine on a cold battlefield surrounded by wounded and dying buddies. God blessed his ministry.

In the less public realm of his life, Bob worked to build the kind of home he had always dreamed of, but had never really had. He wanted a home filled with children, laughter and tenderness, and centered in a shared worship of God. He wanted to be a good husband and daddy. He worked hard at his job and made good money for the times.

Soon he and his wife bought a small house in Oak Ridge. They lived comfortable, respectable lives, faithfully attended church, and Bob began to teach Sunday school. He became a deacon of the church; she sang in the church choir, and almost all their social activities were centered around the church.

Before long their first daughter, Becky, was born. Bob rejoiced in the beautiful little dark-haired, dark-eyed girl. He was a tender, loving daddy, giving his precious baby girl all the affection and attention that he had longed to receive himself as a child. He enjoyed being a father, a husband and a pillar of the church. It was a good time in their lives, and God blessed them.

* * *

Bob was trying to do all that he understood to be the Lord's will for him. He wanted to be a good father, husband, worker and church member, and he thought he was doing a good job of those things. But somehow he never did as well as his wife expected of him. Bob still enjoyed being active in sports. He bowled, pitched horseshoes, played softball and, with all the church activities, he was away from home a good deal. He was enjoying life, and thought everything was going well.

He felt his marriage was as good as the marriages of his friends, maybe better than most. He loved his wife as much as he had ever loved anyone. They did almost everything together, except for his sports activities. They enjoyed playing cards and other games (bridge, Rook, Scrabble) and had a pleasant social life with many friends. They attended church and prayer meetings more faithfully than most, and read the Bible regularly at home. Bob's wife was a choir member, and Bob continued to be active in his lay ministry.

When his wife became pregnant with their second child, she said she wanted a larger house. They decided to build a new home on Robertsville Road, a location closer to the church. Expecting a boy this time, they painted the new baby's room blue and decorated it in a "cowboy" theme. They were ready for a boy to be "big brother" to their sweet Becky. However, God had other ideas. Becky was four years old when her sister, Diane, was born.

They were surprised that God had given them a girl rather the boy they had prepared for, but Bob knew for sure that God doesn't make any mistakes. He thanked God for the gift of this special little girl, who became his "tomboy" and grew to bless their lives in so many ways. Bob considered his girls, Becky and Diane, to be the greatest gifts God had ever given him, and he felt responsible for teaching them about God. They learned how to pray and talk to God almost as soon as they learned to talk to Mommy and Daddy. It was the greatest joy of his life that God allowed Bob to lead these precious children to a knowledge of the saving power of his Lord Jesus Christ. He asked God to bless him in his tender teaching of the girls. He was able, by the power of the Holy Spirit, to tell them how Jesus came—and Jesus comes now—to save us from all fear, worry, anger, hatefulness and from anything in our lives that is not heavenly. He taught the girls that it is God's will for our lives here on earth to be "as it is in heaven"—that is, filled with praise and gratitude and trust and love for the Father who gives us life.

Bob loved playing with his children—and, indeed with all the children of the neighborhood. More than most adults, perhaps, Bob retained a playful, youthful nature. Because of his trust in God's provision for every need of his life, he was not ambitious in the usual sense, and did not, like many men, become a workaholic in an effort to be successful in the business world. Without any great conscious decision on his part, Bob simply placed a greater value on people than on things. Rather than spending long hours at work trying to get ahead in the world, Bob preferred time with his friends in sports activities, at home with his wife and children, or at church praising and glorifying God who had preserved his life in Korea.

Because of his obviously genuine enjoyment of his own children and others in the neighborhood, he became very popular with the kids. Sometimes they would ring the doorbell and ask his wife if Bob could come out and play. He talked to the children about Jesus too, and encouraged them to go to church and take their parents with them.

Bob was trying harder and harder to be a good daddy and husband, but something was going wrong. He realized that he was often mad or otherwise upset for no particular reason. Frequently he found himself uneasy, unhappy with himself and his life. He enjoyed his children, his home, his wife, his church and all his sports activities, but slowly, subtly, something in himself, his marriage and his relationship to the world around him was changing. Something vitally important to his joy in life was missing.

13/ Trouble on the Home Front

Growing up as he did, with parents who never showed affection to each other and seldom to him, Bob had no good role models and no clear pattern for being a good father, husband or lover. There was no sex education available when he was growing up—at home or in the schools. His parents had worked hard and done the best they could for him, but Bob realized there was not much love or affection in their home.

There was never any hugging or kissing in the family. Born with a naturally warm and affectionate nature, Bob nevertheless had little training in how to be a loving husband. He thought he was doing well; he was certainly doing the best he knew how as a lover and husband, but it never seemed to be all that his wife expected or wanted.

His father and mother had often been away from home working or honky tonking. Compared to them, Bob thought he was spending lots of time with his wife and children, despite his many sports activities and church-related responsibilities.

Relative to his own experience growing up with his parents, he was spending a lot of quality time with his family. His parents had never read the Bible at home, and they usually slept in on Sunday mornings rather than take Bob to church, so he tried to do better for his own children. He made a point of having family devotionals and family Bible reading and regular church and Sunday school attendance. Looking back on that time, Bob suspected he went overboard sometimes. Because God and His Word meant so much to him, Bob later saw that he had forced it on his family and on everyone else he knew.

One incident brought this insight home to him in a powerful way. Realizing that her daddy was quite upset at breakfast one morning, his three-year-old, Diane, asked her mother, "What's wrong with Daddy?"

"Daddy is mad because I wouldn't get up and have morning devotionals with him," Mother explained.

Diane looked at Bob, still pouting and mad, and said "Well, it's not helping *him* much is it?"

Bob was forced to laugh and agree with her. Still he continued to push them all in the direction he thought they should go. Toward Jesus. Somehow, in his earnest and determined efforts to "save" everyone he knew, especially his loved ones, he forgot that it really wasn't Bob's job to save them. Jesus would take care of that. It was only Bob's responsibility to tell the Good News.

Like many evangelists before him, Bob became so intensely involved in *pushing* everyone toward the Lord, he forgot that all we need to do is to lift Him up, and *He will draw all men* (and women and children too) to Himself through the power of the Holy Spirit.

* * *

Bob appeared to have everything a man could want. He was successful at work, accepted and liked by his peers. He was in prime physical condition and continued to excel in all the sports he loved. In 1964 and 1967, he won the Class II State Horseshoe Championships, a dream of his since he was a boy watching his father and uncles toss shoes on Sunday afternoons at his Grandfather's house.

Bob had the family he had dreamed of too—a beautiful wife and two bright, healthy and lovely daughters. And he had all of the material things he wanted—a nice home and new car and plenty of money for clothes, vacations and some of the "extras." It's true that his wife still wanted more of the finer things of life, but Bob felt that God had blessed them with all they needed and more.

His wife was from a more ambitious mold, however, and, although she had worked when they were first married, they had agreed that she would not work outside the home after the children were born. She enjoyed being a full-time mother, even though this meant that there was no extra money for many of the little luxuries of life. However, God always provided all that they really needed and more.

So there were no major problems in Bob's life. Still, he was unhappy, and he didn't know why. He began to wonder, "What's wrong with me?" He knew that God wants his children to be happy in this life, as well as in Heaven. Hadn't Jesus said He came that we might have life, and have it more abundantly? And wasn't Bob living the abundant life?

Yet none of the blessings he had received was quite all that he expected or needed. He knew he didn't want more of the material things of life. Yet he realized, as his unhappiness with his life increased month after month, that something was vitally wrong.

Bob began doing things he saw other men do for fun. He joined a health club and started working out regularly. He tried the steam baths, massages, saunas and sun lamps to see if they would make him feel better. He sought pleasure through alcohol—drinking a few beers with his friends after work or after athletic events.

Eventually he started seeing other women, trying to boost his ego with sexual pleasure. As his depression grew, he became willing to do almost anything to make himself feel better. Yet everything he tried only made him feel worse. The more he indulged his flesh, the worse he felt. Bob even began thinking of ending his own life. He was just about as miserable as a man can get—and he didn't even know why.

14/ Renewal

           Although Bob was moving farther and farther from God, his Lord never moved away from him. Jesus was with him and kept reminding him, through the scripture that rang over and over in his puzzled mind, that the key to a fuller life was close at hand.

> *I am come that they might have life, and have it more abundantly.* **(John 10:10)**

"What does that mean?" Bob asked himself over and over in his misery. "Now that I have all this abundance, and can do just about anything I want to do, I'm more miserable than I've ever been in my life. Surely God doesn't want me to live like this."

One day while Bob was at work in his office, with at least twenty other people busy at their own tasks all around him, he laid his unhappy head down on his desk and prayed a prayer of desperation:

"Lord Jesus, I *know* that You love me. I *know* that You died to save me from my sin. I *know* that Your Word says that if I confess my sins You will forgive me. **(I John 1:9)**. Lord, I am coming now to Your throne of grace. I am coming boldly, as You have taught us to come in the name of Jesus, confessing my sins of adultery, drunkenness, hatred, unforgivingness and selfishness. And I confess to You that I have forgotten about Your sacrifice and tried to save myself. I have been puffed up with pride and conceit because of all the blessings You have given me. I started thinking I was better than other people. I was so full of pride that I thought I was the only Christian, the best Christian, the only person in the world who was even trying to be good. I thought I *was* good. I have carried old resentments against the way my mama and daddy lived and the way they raised me, without affection and without the nurture of Your Church. I have been blaming them for my sins, for my unhappiness.

"I confess that I can do nothing without You. I cannot overcome my sinful nature. I can't be the good father and good husband that I want to be, without You and the power of the Holy Spirit within me. I am asking You to cleanse me now from all my sins, just as Your Word says You will do. And now that I am cleansed by Your Power, I ask You, Lord Jesus, to take control of my life, to live in me and to enable me to do Your will and good pleasure. I yield myself completely to You. You are the potter; I am the clay. Take me and mold me and make me what You would have me to be, for Your honor and glory forever. In Jesus' name I pray all this. Amen."

Bob opened his eyes. He didn't know how long he had been pouring out his heart to God. He raised his head and looked around. The other graphic artists were still intent on their own work. No one noticed him at all. No one knew or cared that he had passed through a crisis in his life. No one recognized that anything at all unusual had happened.

Bob went back to his own work. He felt nothing, not even relief. In the days that followed, he struggled to believe that God had heard his desperate prayer, but he detected no change in his feelings of hopelessness or in the circumstances of his life.

He noticed only one small difference in himself to suggest God had heard his prayer and was beginning to take charge of his life. He suddenly had a renewed desire to read the Bible. And, as he began reading the Word again, he couldn't get enough of it. Passages he had never particularly noticed before suddenly came alive for him. God's Word, and the parables and lessons there, were more real, more exciting, than he had ever noticed before. He experienced a deeper understanding than ever before of so much that he read now. Gradually, Bob began to feel better. He grew hopeful, and his faith grew stronger that God WAS, in fact, answering his prayer.

He bought a copy of a new translation of the Bible that had just been published—*The Living Bible*. The ancient scriptures had been paraphrased in modern everyday English language. Bob loved it. He could hardly put it down, in fact. *The Living Bible* made the scriptures easier to read and understand and simplified the very thoughts of God so that even Bob, a simple country boy (as he still thought of himself), could understand them. He read:

> *The law of the Lord is perfect, converting the soul. The testimony of the Lord is sure, making wise the simple.* (Psalm 19:7)

And he discovered this passage:

> *God has deliberately chosen to use ideas the world considers foolish and of little worth in order to shame those people considered by the world as wise and great. He has chosen a plan despised by the world, counted as nothing at all, and used it to bring down to nothing those the world considers great, so that no one anywhere can ever brag in the presence of God.* (Corinthians 1:27-29)

Bob realized anew that it is from God alone that we have our life through Christ Jesus. He showed us His Plan of Salvation. He alone makes us acceptable to God by the sacrifice of death on the cross. He, through Jesus, made us pure and holy and gave Himself to purchase our salvation. Bob began to understand all over again, and more than ever before, why the scriptures teach us:

> *If anyone is going to boast, let him boast only of what God has done.* (I Corinthians 1:31)

Bob began to see that his depression had its roots in his own pridefulness, in his gradual movement away from relying totally on God to relying totally on Bob.

As his eager reading of the Word spoke to his heart and directed him back to placing all his hope and trust and faith in God, rather than in the pleasures of the world, Bob gradually began to feel better about himself and about life. But God was not yet finished with Bob's spiritual renewal.

15/ A Twist of Fate

*O*ne Saturday morning, after Bob had finished mowing his lawn and was putting the lawn mower in the basement, the telephone rang. Ordinarily he never bothered to answer it, since it almost always was for his wife or two daughters. But, as the phone kept on ringing, Bob assumed no one was upstairs to answer it. He picked up the receiver at the same moment that his wife also answered the phone upstairs.

Before he could say anything, he heard words that would change his life forever.

"Hello, darling," a male voice spoke.

"I'm so glad to hear your voice," came his wife's answer. "I love you."

"I love you too. Can we be together today?"

"I want to be with you," she replied. "I miss you."

As the man responded to this declaration, Bob recognized the voice talking love to his wife as that of a man he had thought of for years as a friend.

Bob was speechless. He tried to speak, to protest this new twist of fate in his life, but he couldn't. His heart was in his mouth. It took several minutes before he gained enough composure to talk into the phone.

"I know God can forgive you," he said, with hurt ringing in his voice. "I don't know whether I can or not." Then he hung up the phone and walked upstairs, passing right by his wife, who still clung to the phone.

Bob went to the bedroom he and his wife shared and took a shower, put on clean clothes, and then went back to the room where his wife, in hushed tones, was still talking on the phone. He stood there for a few minutes, then went out the front door toward his car. Putting down the receiver, she followed him out.

"What are you going to do?" she asked.

"I just don't know," Bob answered, the hurt still sounding in his voice. "I'm going to drive around for a while and think."

"Do you want me to leave?"

"If you want to stay, you will have to give up Jim," Bob said. "You can't stay and still contrive to see him."

Bob felt so bad that he hurt all over—all through. He was sick, crushed. He wished that he could die right there, right then.

His wife said, "If I decide to stay with you, will you be able to forgive me? Or will you always hold this over my head?"

Bob suddenly remembered the story in John's Gospel of the woman taken in the very act of adultery. When the Scribes and Pharisees brought her to Jesus, wanting to stone her to death, Jesus said:

'All right, hurl stones at her until she dies.
But only he who never sinned may throw
the first.' (John 8:7)

Then Jesus stood up again and said to her,
'Where are your accusers? Didn't even
one of them condemn you?' 'No sir,' she
said. And Jesus said, 'Neither do I. Go and
sin no more.' (John 8:10-11)

As this went through Bob's mind, he told his wife that God's Word teaches that if we don't forgive others, then neither will we be forgiven.

Then he asked her to forgive him, too. He confessed that he had also committed the sin of adultery. He told her that he forgave her and, with God's help, would also try hard to forget it, to put it behind them. They cried together and promised forgiveness to each other.

Bob left the house then. He needed to be alone, to meditate and pray. He asked God to help him do the right thing. He recognized that God had allowed him to pick up the telephone at the very moment he did, so that his wife's affair would be revealed to him.

Suddenly he saw, more vividly than ever, the ugly, hurtful side of adultery. Though his own adulterous affairs had meant only a moment's pleasure, a sensual gratification of his sexual desires, he now recognized, through his own pain, why God's Word forbids adultery. It is not for God's benefit that He has set forth this law, but for *our* benefit. God knows that adultery can bring about great pain, guilt, sadness, sickness, perhaps years of suffering, and even death. Adultery can destroy every good thing in a marriage relationship. As it is written:

> *But the man who commits adultery is an utter fool, for he destroys his own soul.* (Proverbs 6:32)

Bob asked God again to forgive him of his sin of adultery. He begged God to help him never to hurt anyone as he had just been hurt by knowledge of his wife's cheating. He humbly asked God's mercy and cleansing, confessing all his shameful deeds. He felt that God did forgive him and that God would also enable him to forgive his wife.

Having done this, Bob drove directly to where his wife's lover worked. He walked into the office and, by the power of the Holy Spirit, he felt no anger. He had no desire to hurt Jim or his family. He understood, because God had given him this understanding through his own experience, that Jim had been deceived by Satan, just as Bob had been deceived by Satan.

Jim asked him to wait until he had finished with his last customer, then he received him into his office, where he asked Bob to forgive him.

"I'll do anything for you, anything you ask," Jim pleaded. "Just please don't tell my wife."

Bob told him he already had forgiven the adulterous pair.

"If you want to do something for me, then start going to church regularly," Bob said. "Take your wife and children. And read your Bible; it's the only thing of lasting value in this life."

Bob realized that God was the only answer for all of them—for himself, his wife and the girls, and for Jim and his wife and children. More than ever before, Bob understood that God is the only answer for all the world's problems, the only solution for the sins and failures of humankind.

* * *

Although Bob and his wife had cried and prayed together and forgiven each other, Bob struggled daily with the demons of jealousy. He knew that Satan's power of temptation is strong. He realized his wife would love to have the more luxurious lifestyle and the material things of life that Jim could offer and he couldn't. He knew there was still the possibility, and even probability, that she and Jim would continue their affair. He knew she did not love him as a wife should love her husband and he was afraid that maybe she did love Jim.

He tried to overcome the jealousy, but anytime he called home and his wife wasn't there, he'd think, *They're together.* If he called home and the line was busy, he would think, *They're talking love talk to each other.*

Satan, who employs all the deadly tools of jealousy— distrust, suspicion and fear—was fast gaining control of Bob's life. Reflecting on this time, Bob later said, "Satan was really having fun with me. I had given up all my pleasure-seeking sins and I was working full-time on sins that were making me miserable. Pretty dumb, huh?"

* * *

Bob began to recognize and to confess these miserable sins to his Lord every day, and he began to get back into reading and trusting in the Word of God. As always, the Word of the Lord comforted him and covered him with a circle of peace, even in the midst of this devastating situation. He cast all his cares upon the Lord, as Jesus asks us to do in **I Peter 5:7.**

He surrendered his wife and Jim and their affair up to the Lord. He surrendered his children to the Lord. And, as time went by, he was again delivered from the torment of fear. He was delivered from the tortures of jealousy, anxiety and suspicion. As Bob practiced casting his cares upon the Lord daily, he began to be open to receiving the peace of God that is promised in His Word—the wonderful peace that passes all human understanding.

Those who have experienced this peace, and there are millions who have, know that such peace has nothing to do with what is going on in the world, nothing to do with human relationships, nothing to do with the body's state of health or wealth or status. It has only to do with the glorious peace and power of God's transcending love.

Resting in the arms of his Lord Jesus, and nurtured daily by His Word of Peace, Bob gradually became contented, happy and carefree. Nothing changed at home or in his relationship with his wife. She didn't suddenly start loving Bob again. In fact, he had reason to believe that she and Jim continued their affair just as before, despite their promises to him. But even if this were true, it was no longer a source of daily torment for Bob. Led by the Spirit of God, Bob concentrated on loving his wife in an unselfish way, as he realized he never really had done before.

He tried in every way to win her love again. He made every effort to be a good husband to her and a good father to their girls. He gave up the time-consuming sports activities that he had enjoyed so much.

Even though he had been a state champion at horseshoes, he quit going to tournaments. Likewise he gave up bowling, softball, fishing and hunting. He gave up every activity that kept him away from home.

He bought books on love-making, and sought to become a better and more sensitive lover to his wife. He bought books on child-rearing and Christian parenting, trying to become a better daddy to Becky and Diane. And he kept on reading the Word of God and growing stronger in his faith.

* * *

Strangely, as Bob grew stronger and kinder and more at peace with himself and with God, his wife grew more unhappy. The better he treated her, the more miserable she became. In an amorous mood one night, Bob rubbed her shoulders and, when she appeared to enjoy it, he increased his efforts to a more seductive massage. But she suddenly rejected his advances and turned away. Bob didn't react by getting angry. He just continued the massage in a way that would be acceptable to her, feeling real love for her, real concern for her comfort, her pleasure, her enjoyment, rather than seeking only to satisfy his own sexual desires. Then he turned over and went to sleep, filled with peace and contentment.

The next morning, she turned to him and began to talk about their relationship and her expectations from life.

"Bob, you're a fine man," she said. "I love you as if you were my brother, but no longer as a husband. I want you to find someone to love who will also love you and respond to you in return. You need and deserve that kind of wife, but I cannot respond to you as you want me to.

"You've taught me what a good wife should be," she continued, "but I no longer want to be your wife. I want to be a good wife to Jim. Divorce me and find someone else."

Realizing that he had, indeed, lost her love forever, Bob agreed to think seriously about a divorce. He went to see his pastor and told him that his wife was in love with another man and wanted a divorce.

"I don't believe in divorce," Bob explained. "I believe what the Bible says about it, and I want to do only what Jesus wants me to do."

Some ministers would have immediately condemned the idea of divorce and stated flatly that there should be no divorce under any circumstances. But Bob's pastor was a minister of God's love and a man of rare wisdom. He replied to Bob's broken-hearted inquiry by teaching him that God is indeed a God of love, and that God hates adultery and God hates divorce because they are hurtful and sinful.

"But God has provided for our sins through Christ Jesus; in Him our sins can be and *are* forgiven. God does hate sin; he hates anything that is not peace and joy and goodness and love in the lives of His children. But if we live with someone and are in constant misery, that is also a sin in God's eyes.

"It breaks God's heart when he sees us unable to love and nurture and forgive one another and live in the joyful harmony for which he has designed us as man and woman joined in holy matrimony," the wise pastor continued.

"It has been God's plan from the beginning—from the very moment that he created Eve to be a companion and helpmate for Adam—that a man should have a wife and a woman should have a husband, and the two should be in such a joyfully close and loving relationship that they become as one flesh, one mind, one spirit.

"This is what God wants a marriage relationship to be. Because God loves us, He has given us these Biblical instructions and laws designed to bring us the peace and joy that He planned for us to have. But, because He knows and understands our selfish and sinful nature, He has given permission for divorce if this loving relationship is broken, as when a wife or husband commits adultery **(Matthew 5:32)**.

"Even in the Old Testament, God provided that if a man doesn't want to remain married to his wife, he may write a letter of divorcement. Then she may marry again." **(Deuteronomy 24:1-2)**

Bob's pastor explained that divorce is a sin, but it isn't an unpardonable sin. If we confess our sin, God is *always* faithful to forgive us and to cleanse us from all unrighteousness. **(I John 1:9)**

The pastor said, "Bob, if you divorce and later fall in love again, you will want to be married again. When that happens, remember that your past sins, those which you have confessed to God and asked him to forgive with repentance in your heart and mind, those sins are forever forgiven and forgotten by God.

"God never holds a grudge and, in fact, his own Holy Word says that forgiven sins are 'remembered no more.' So if you decide to marry again, it will be just the same as the first time in God's sight.

"Your past is forgotten, your past sins covered forever from the sight of God by the blood of His Son, Jesus.

"Of course," the pastor added, "Even though the sins are forgiven and forgotten by God, there may still be consequences here on this earth. In the case of divorce, the consequences include the pain of separation from the lives of your children and the loss of your home and your wife. If you remarry, there will be the complicated relationships between wife and ex-wife, children and stepchildren, grandchildren and step-grandchildren, in-laws and ex-in-laws. It isn't any wonder that our loving Father decreed that we should have only one wife. He knows the consequences for us if we do otherwise."

* * *

Bob thought long and seriously about all the pastor had said. It was now four years since the painful day when he had first discovered that his wife and Jim were lovers. Bob's marriage had continued through all those years.

It had not been a "heavenly" relationship as God wills a marriage to be, but it had provided a home and a caring environment for the girls. Bob had felt happy and contented in the marriage, because he was being a faithful husband and a good daddy, and because he knew that he was doing what God wanted him to do. He was not happy that his wife loved someone else more than she loved him; he wasn't happy that she wanted a divorce. But even after all they had been through, Bob felt more love for her than he had felt even at the beginning of their marriage.

He had come to realize that for most of his life he had really loved himself more than he had loved anyone else. He was deeply sorry that he had been unable to love his wife as fully as she had needed and wanted.

In the time since that realization, he had surrendered his life to the will of God and allowed the Holy Spirit of God, the very Spirit of Love, to fill him. He knew that now Jesus was in control of his life, and Bob sought to show, in a way that would be pleasing to Him, this love for his wife.

Bob was determined that, come what may, she and the children would be well-provided for. He finally told her he would never leave her or the children unless she had someone to provide and care for them. Bob agreed with her, however, that if Jim did, in fact, fulfill his promise to divorce his own wife and marry her, then, and only then, would Bob grant a divorce.

Jim and his wife did divorce, eventually, and Jim showed Bob real proof—in the form of a will making Bob's wife and the girls beneficiaries—that he intended to marry her and provide for the girls. Faced with this final, certain sign of love and commitment between his wife and his former friend, Bob at last agreed to a divorce.

There was no hatred in his heart toward her or Jim. Bob realized they loved each other. But there was great pain at losing his wife, his daughters and his home. He understood that these were the painful and inevitable consequences of past sins, his own sins as well as hers and Jim's, just as his pastor had explained years before.

* * *

After the divorce, Bob moved to an apartment in Knoxville and began to build a new life. He wanted a fresh start. He visited other churches, learned about other denominations, and prayed for God's guidance in finding a new church. He visited the Church of God, Methodist, Episcopal, Presbyterian, Catholic, Seventh Day Adventist and Baptist churches, and found there were some things he liked about them all.

Having grown up in a Baptist church, however, he still was most comfortable there. He discovered that a former acquaintance was now minister of education at the Central Baptist Church in Bearden. This man had been minister of education at Robertsville Baptist, the church Bob had attended with his wife for all of their married life, and where Bob had taught several Sunday school classes and served as superintendent of the Sunday school.

When the minister learned that Bob was attending Central Baptist, he came to visit him and asked if he would consider starting a singles ministry at the Bearden church.

At that time, there were few if any singles classes in Knoxville churches, but the clergy were becoming aware of the need to minister to widowed and divorced single adults. Knowing that Bob was a good teacher and a strong Christian who had recently gone through the trauma of divorce, the minister thought he would be a good person to start this new ministry.

Bob saw that God was offering him the opportunity to work through the pain and depression of his own divorce by starting a ministry that would help others in the same situation. He prayed about it, and soon he found that he really wanted to do it. He knew that God was leading him to do it, and he knew that if God wants you to do something, He will give you the desire to do it and the means to do it, and He will bless your efforts. So Bob joined Central Baptist in starting what may have been the first singles ministry in the city. The class began in 1971. Bob was forty years old.

There were only a few single adult members in the class at first, but God blessed the ministry, and soon others joined them. Sunday by Sunday, as the class grew, Bob felt that Jesus was using him to share His Word—the Good News—that God wants us, His children, married or divorced, to be delivered from depression, loneliness, temptation, fear, worry, anger, sickness and death—all the evils of sin in this world. And God wants us to enjoy all the fruits of the spirit instead—love, joy, peace, health and harmony. It was a very exciting time.

Bob praised God for filling the emptiness of his life with this wonderful opportunity to grow spiritually and to help others grow too. He really understood the humiliation, the feelings of worthlessness and hopelessness that come to those who are divorced after months or years of what they thought was a good marriage. He loved sharing what his wise pastor at Robertsville had taught him about God's love and forgiveness and how it's never too late for a joyful life, because God always gives us another chance.

16/ Rising from the Ashes

About this time, Bob was really blessed by a book he read, *Prison to Praise,* by Merlin Carothers. The whole book was based on this text:

No matter what happens, always be thankful, for this is God's will for you who belong to Jesus Christ. (I Thessalonians 5:18)

Bob had started practicing this idea of giving thanks *in everything*, even before his divorce. He had even thanked God that his wife wanted a divorce. He thanked God that He could take anything, any situation, no matter how bad, and make something good out of it. After reading Carothers' book, he worked even harder at praising and thanking God for taking all of our sins, failures and problems, and using them for our good and His glory.

Even though he realized it had not been God's will that he and his wife divorce, Bob saw that God was taking that situation and that experience to help him and to help many others draw closer to God and find new meaning and purpose for their lives. Though Satan had done his best to destroy all hope and joy, through the destruction of homes and families, by divorce, yet God was reaching out to His children in their loneliness and despair and drawing them into His own loving arms.

Yet, in spite of the joy and excitement of the growing new singles ministry, Bob was often lonely and sometimes depressed. He had never lived alone in his whole life, and he didn't like it at all. He really had no desire for another wife or child who would grow to love him and then might be taken from him. That would be like having his heart torn out a second time. He had learned that it is not easy to be a good husband and certainly not easy to be a good parent.

He didn't want to marry again, but he liked women and enjoyed female companionship. As the teacher of young single women, he was also uncomfortable on those occasions when they displayed a greater regard for him than they should.

Because he sincerely felt and expressed concern and understanding for them, and because he offered to them the love of God, trying to show them God's tender, forgiving side, he was concerned that some of the women would seek Bob's love rather than the love of Jesus that he was trying to pour out to them. He was also a man, and was aware that he was subject to the temptations of any other man.

Many of the sweet women were so hungry for love and attention, so vulnerable to the attentions of any man, that it was sometimes a temptation hard to resist. Yet the Lord did provide Bob the strength to resist taking advantage, and he was never tempted beyond his power to resist.

Often Bob would go to the altar and pray. He asked the Lord to bless his ministry to the wounded single adults; he asked God to enable him to resist Satan's temptation to go beyond the loving teacher relationship with the young women in his class. He praised God for providing for his every need, even in the midst of his loneliness and pain.

Gradually Bob realized that he needed a helpmate and he went to the Lord in prayer, saying "Lord, if You want me to continue in the service of helping single adults, including single women, please send me a wife to be a helpmate in this ministry and in my life. I need a wife."

There was only one woman he was even remotely interested in romantically. He had met her during hospital visitation for the church. Her name was Margaret, and she was recovering from a bad automobile accident. He learned that she was a member of Robertsville Baptist Church and a lovely lady. Bob enjoyed talking with her, and he could tell she enjoyed their conversations too. But he learned she was married. Bob knew her husband only slightly, but he knew that he was in poor health resulting from the alcoholism that afflicted him.

After two or three visits, Bob also realized that Margaret was not a spirit-filled Christian. He started teaching her about Jesus, assuring her that our Lord wants us to be healed and happy, and he provides the Holy Spirit to make that possible, no matter our lives' circumstances. He taught her that God loved her, personally, and that He wanted her to praise Him in everything, even in the midst of all the misery of her physical recovery and her life with an alcoholic husband.

* * *

Margaret was eager to hear the Good News. Her faith was renewed through the guidance of the Holy Spirit's teaching, through Bob, and she began coming to church regularly.

Later, after Margaret's husband died of his many ailments, Margaret's friendship with Bob began to grow and express itself in new ways. Margaret already loved Bob, as one Christian loves another, for leading her to a closer relationship with her Lord. And Bob already loved her, as the spirit of God's love flowed through him to minister to her.

Yet now, he allowed himself to recognize things about his attraction to her, things he had pushed from his mind before. He allowed himself to recognize consciously what he already knew subconsciously—that she was a pretty woman, and that she was fun to be with. Bob began to think that she could be the helpmate he had asked God to send into his life.

Before long, he asked her out, and they began dating. Margaret had two grown children, a boy and a girl, and no desire for more. Both of her children were married, and

Bob liked them both. More and more he felt that Margaret was the woman God wanted him to marry. They enjoyed each other's company more and more often.

Their relationship quickly turned into a "whirlwind romance," with everything working toward bringing them together. Margaret needed a husband to provide for her, and Bob needed a wife and helpmate in his ministry. They needed each other and accepted their love and marriage as gifts from God. Yet they were concerned about what people would say if they married, since her husband's death was still relatively recent. They really wanted God's will to be done in their lives and in the lives of their children, and they went to talk with their pastor about the possibility of getting married. Their pastor told them that no matter how long they waited, the talkers would still talk. With this advice in mind, they accepted their feelings that it was God's will that they be joined as man and wife. They got married.

It was a very happy time for both of them. God blessed them and used them to bless others in many ways. Margaret was indeed a wonderful helpmate in the singles ministry. They became more and more involved in that work and in other ministries within the church.

Bob loved Margaret and her children. She also got along well with his children. Those first few years were the happiest times of Bob's life. He knew that God had indeed given him another chance for a joyful and satisfying family life.

Margaret loved Bob more, it seemed, than anyone ever had—even more than his mother. Margaret was good to him and to his children as well as her own. She spoiled all of them with her kindness, and willingly gave of her time and effort to them all. Their home was a happy, joyful place. Bob felt that, at last, he had gained the "heavenly" home that God wants each of us to have in our marriage—a relaxing atmosphere of total, unconditional love and acceptance.

Bob loved coming home from work to Margaret. She was a wonderful cook, and she enjoyed making big, home-cooked meals and having all of the children join them for dinner. Any dish they hungered for, Margaret would cook for them. Anything they wanted, she tried to give them, and she loved spoiling them all.

In the church ministry too, Margaret was a wonderful helpmate for Bob. God used them in miraculous ways. People were led to Jesus, given mental and physical healing, led to new and fulfilling Christian lives and new marriages. Many were filled with the fruits of the Holy Spirit, love and forgiveness.

As the ministry grew, the demands on Bob's time grew also. It was tiring and difficult, while holding a full-time job, to spend so many hours being teacher and counselor, leading the many broken-hearted, single adults toward the healing power of Jesus.

Bob still spent many hours working with single women. Some were depressed, physically sick and often mentally and spiritually sick as well due to divorce, involvement with married men, alcoholism, drugs, abortions, suicide attempts and every kind of sorrowful, sinful problem that Satan had sent into their lives.

Margaret was helpful, supportive, understanding and, miraculously, was not jealous of the many hours he spent in this ministry. Bob considered himself to be blessed among men. He realized that he could not have carried out this ministry without Margaret's support and encouragement. These were wonderful, joyous years, filled with God's richest blessings.

* * *

But whenever God is using us and blessing us most fully with His joy, Satan is hard at work thinking up ways to attack us and divert us from carrying out the will of God. Swiftly and boldly, or slowly and insidiously, the Devil will attack us with sickness, aggravations, condemnations, lies, and all the many other evils at his command. He will do anything to rob us of our joy. Satan wants us to be miserable. He wants to bring failure and discredit to every effort we make on God's behalf. He wants us to curse God and die, so that we will belong to him (Satan) forevermore. Satan brings disease into healthy bodies; he brings disharmony into happy homes; he brings lies and misunderstandings and hurt feelings to destroy close family relationships; he brings criticism and defensiveness to destroy loving and supportive marriages. Satan steals our joy, kills our love and destroys all that is good in our lives if we are not constantly on guard against him. God knows that Satan will continue to attack us again and again so long as we live. As God's Holy Word has warned us:

> *Be careful—watch out for attacks from*
> *Satan, your great enemy. He prowls*
> *around like a hungry, roaring lion,*
> *looking for some victim to tear apart.*
> **(I Peter 5:8)**

Yet Our Lord has provided for us in every way. If we keep looking to Him, keep our lives and our spirits filled with the nourishment of His Word, we have the promise of victory over all that Satan can devise.

> *So give yourselves humbly to God. Resist*
> *the devil and he will flee from you.*
> **(James 4:7)**

Despite knowing God's Word and having the great salvation of the Lord Jesus, Margaret and Bob, like all of us, are continually under siege from Satan. Margaret's health problems, her back pain, arthritis and other ills get worse year by year. Bob continues his lifelong battle against fear of not being good enough, of being misunderstood or forgotten, of growing old or disabled and being left without the love of a wife and children and without a "heavenly" home on earth and, most of all, fear that he might somehow fail to carry out the will of God for his life.

Yet, despite that fear, Bob continues to hold fast to the love of God, which is manifest most fully to us in the life of Christ Jesus and in His Word. Bob continues to share the Good News with all who will listen. In reading the Word, he continues to find comfort and relief from fear. He ministers daily to all of God's children crossing his path, young or old, rich or poor; from prominent and successful business executives to hardened murderers imprisoned for life; from neglected and abandoned children to disillusioned and unhappy wives and husbands.

He continues, in his quiet and faithful way, to fulfill his responsibilities, as God gives him the wisdom to understand those responsibilities.

Daily he seeks guidance and sustenance and spiritual understanding from reading God's Holy Word. Daily he prays, asking God's healing intervention for those who are mentally or physically ill; daily he teaches, and demonstrates as he teaches, the unending and unconditional love and forgiveness of God for a needy and sinful humankind. Daily he fights the temptations of this world. Daily he picks up his cross and follows Jesus; daily he thanks God for all the circumstances of his life, praising Him for every circumstance and holding fast to the promises of His Word, which are many and precious to his heart. The Bible says:

> *But they that wait upon the Lord shall renew their strength. They shall mount up with wings like eagles; they shall run and not be weary; they shall walk and not faint.* **(Isaiah 40:31)**

And in another scripture:

> *... and he will give (these things) to you if you give him first place in your life and live as he wants you to.* (Matthew 6:33)

And again:

> *Be delighted with the Lord. Then he will give you all your heart's desires.* (Psalms 37:4)

And yet again:

> *Ask ... and you will receive, and your cup of joy will overflow.* (John 16:24)

This joy of which Jesus spoke is the joy of fulfilling our own special purpose that He created for us in His Great Plan. It is Bob's greatest joy to simply make himself available to his Lord every day. As Bob expresses it, "I think it's wonderful that I can go into my Boss's office every morning and ask Him directly, 'What do You want me to do for You today?' That's wonderful!" It is Bob's greatest desire that his created purpose in life should be to win souls and be a blessing to others.

Yet even our Lord Jesus was not always considered a blessing by the people of His time in history. He was often treated as a curse rather than a blessing by many of His own family, neighbors and religious leaders. If Jesus had measured his success in life by the number of people He met who loved and appreciated Him and considered Him a blessing, He might have been filled with misery to think of all those who failed to receive the tender love and healing and forgiveness that He offered as a free gift from God.

But Jesus understood that God had sent Him to be a living sacrifice, to suffer rejection and pain and sorrow, even for a sinful and unaccepting world. Even so, God is continuing to teach Bob, and through him many others, that He is able to direct all the circumstances of our lives—the wonderful, joyful, loving moments, and the painful moments of rejection, misunderstanding, failure and fear—and that He is able to use all these circumstances for our ultimate good and His ultimate glory.

The Lord is continuing to work in Bob's life, while preparing for him that Heavenly Home, not of this earth, that Bob has always longed to have.

Living by faith is never easy. God is teaching Bob, and teaching others through him, that it is easier, far easier, to be a battle hero standing in a hail of enemy gunfire than to live a heroically sacrificial life through day after ordinary day of aggravations and criticisms and complaints.

It is, in fact, humanly impossible for any man to continue long to love and to serve and to sacrifice without gratitude or appreciation or praise. But, as it is promised in His Word:

With God, everything is possible.
(Mark 10:27)

We also know that:

Abiding love surrounds those who trust in the Lord. (Psalm 32:10)

Most importantly, we have glad tidings of God's great power to care for His children:

He forgives all my sins. He heals me. He ransoms me from hell. He surrounds me with lovingkindness and tender mercies. He fills my life with good things. My youth is renewed like the eagle's! (Psalm 103:3-5).

Bob continues to share these wonderful promises of life abundant and everlasting wherever he goes, and to share the Good News with all he meets. It is Bob's hope and his prayer that by sharing these experiences of his life, others may come to know and love the Lord Jesus Christ.

To God be the Glory, forever and ever.

Amen.

Author's Note

"FREEDOM ISN'T FREE ..."

These words are etched deeply in the black granite wall of the Korean War Memorial recently dedicated in Washington, D.C. The words are flanked by evidence of their truth: portraits of 2,000 of the more than 54,000 American service personnel who died during that war. Those soldiers died fighting to preserve the freedom of a foreign people in a foreign nation, but also to preserve our own freedom, for the earth is only a small planet. When freedom is lost for any, it is lost for all.

Also reflected in the wall's highly polished surface are the faces of visitors: family members, friends and comrades of those who died and those who come to remember and to honor those who paid freedom's ultimate price. Bob Durham, the man whose life is sketched in this book, was among those who attended the dedication of the Memorial in July 1995. He and his Marine buddy, Griff, along with other members of "Charlie Company" (Company C, First Battalion, Fifth Marines), and thousands of other men and women who served in the Korean War, walked the wall and saw their own faces reflected there, mingling with those of the slain. Freedom isn't free; the Korean War changed all of their lives forever. They all paid a part of freedom's cost.

During the years of our friendship, Bob has shared his memories of the Korean War and his extraordinary experiences there. The stories of his heroic actions were told not with pride in his heroism but with a sort of wonder that God would enable him to serve bravely and honorably despite his fear, and with a deep sense of gratitude for having personally experienced God's wonderful protective power.

As our friendship deepened, Bob shared stories of his childhood, which included both poverty and neglect, and his experiences after the Korean War: the breakup of his marriage and loss of his home and children. Shining through all of these stories was the golden thread of faith: faith in a God both powerful and compassionate, a God who loves and stands with him through all the sorrows and hardships of life. A God who is able and who does use ALL things for good in the life of a man who truly loves Him.

Bob's faith affected me, too. As I watched Bob sharing the "Good News" with every person he met along life's path, I encouraged him to share his testimony in a broader way, through publication of a book telling his life story. At last, with retirement, time became available for Bob to write down his memories in a letter for his grandchildren. That letter has provided the basis for this manuscript.

To guard the privacy and protect the feelings of his first wife, Bob has requested that her given name not be used and that the name of her second husband be changed. Other than these alterations, the stories are presented here as Bob told them. Our prayer is that God will use this effort for His Glory; that other Christians might be encouraged to see God's power working in every circumstance of their own lives, and that those who are not yet Christians might wonder at a God so caring, so faithful, and so powerful, and seek to know Him.

Jeanne Hall
September 25, 1995
Knoxville, Tennessee